Instant Pot Cooking

WHEN YOU'RE UNDER PRESSURE

CENTENNIAL KITCHEN®

CENTENNIAL BOOKS

Instant Pot Cooking

WHEN YOU'RE UNDER PRESSURE

CONTENTS

66

108

94

132

26

12

52

ONE-POT WONDERS

In a hurry to get a meal on the table? That's where the Instant Pot becomes your best friend. Part slow cooker, part stovetop skillet, part steamer and part oven, its combination of high pressure and heat means meals that once took hours can now be dished out in about 30 minutes or less. Plus, it's safe, easy to clean and not a big space waster, and can be used to make everything from beverages and beans to soups, stews, roasts, pasta—even dessert. In other words, it's the perfect addition to your kitchen, especially on time-crunched days.

Many of you have already discovered the joys of cooking with this programmable multicooker and are looking to explore all of its features. Or maybe you recently received one as a gift, and you're ready to learn how to get started preparing delicious dishes with it. Whatever your level of experience with the Instant Pot, this book has you covered.

Starting with a quick overview of the features available and a review of the basic settings, we take you from breakfast to dessert with mouthwatering recipes for an amazing range of dishes and drinks that you'll have on the table in a flash (some take a little longer but we promise, it's worth it!). We've got more than 150 foolproof recipes for basics like perfect rice, hard-boiled eggs and marinara sauce, as well as more fanciful fare like beef stroganoff, poached mahi-mahi, chicken piccata, mocha lava cakes and pumpkin creme brulee. So what are you waiting for? Read on, then plug in your Instant Pot and get cooking!

Chocolate Chip
Mini Muffins,
page 140

LEARNING THE BASICS

ALL INSTANT POTS—NO MATTER THE MODEL—COME WITH A USER MANUAL THAT WILL FILL YOU IN ON THE FUNDAMENTALS OF USING YOUR NEW KITCHEN TOOL, BUT THIS QUICK RUNDOWN WILL GET YOU STARTED.

What to Expect

■ When you plug your pot in, the display will read Ultra, the default setting for pressure-cooking at high for 30 minutes. You can adjust the cooking program by turning the knob. Options typically include Pressure Cook (Manual), Soup/Broth, Meat/Stew, Bean/Chili, Steam, Slow Cook, Sauté, Warm, Rice, Porridge, Multigrain, Cake, Egg, Sterilize, Yogurt and Ultra. Each of these programs has a default cook time, though you can also select a time as well as temperature and high or low pressure (if applicable to the program). When you have chosen the desired cooking function and adjusted the time, just push start.

If you need to start over, press the Cancel button.

Keep in Mind

■ Close the pressure release valve for all cooking functions except Slow Cook, Sauté and Yogurt.
■ For both the Sauté and Slow Cook functions, there are three temperature settings: low, medium and high.
NOTE Although these instructions are written for the Ultra 10-in-1 Multi-Use Programmable Pressure Cooker, they are easily adaptable to the Duo 7-in-1 Multi-Use Programmable Pressure Cooker (or even older models). Low/medium/high in these instructions correspond to less/normal/more on older Instant Pot models.

Pressure Cooker Functions

Each of the preset pressure-cooking programs defaults to high pressure, with the exception of Rice, which defaults to low pressure. Each preset program also has a default cook time, but can be adjusted to less or more time.

The Slow Cook Function

The Slow Cook function defaults to a 4-hour cook time on medium heat, but both the time and temperature can be adjusted up or down. Most slow-cook recipes call for high temperature ("more" on older models). This temperature level is the equivalent of medium-high if there were such a setting on a stand-alone

Instant Pots come in several sizes, ranging from 3 to 10 quarts.

slow cooker, so the timings fall between what would be low and high on a regular slow cooker.

The Sauté Function

You don't need to set a cook time for the Sauté function, but it automatically shuts off after 30 minutes. Medium-heat setting is the most frequently used. Use high to quickly sear a piece of meat. Use low to gently simmer or reduce a sauce.

The Yogurt Function

The program for homemade yogurt involves a two-stage process—first to boil and cool down the milk, then to incubate the yogurt for a minimum of 8 hours after the live cultures are added.

Basic Operation & Guidelines

1 To open the lid, grab the handle and rotate the lid counterclockwise about 10 degrees. A chime will then sound.

2 The stainless steel inner pot can be removed for cleaning and so you can easily read the volume-level markings on the inside. Be sure the outside of the pot is clean before you place it in the cooker.

3 When pressure-cooking, be sure the total amount of food and liquid doesn't go above the level indicated on the inner pot. It's recommended that the inner pot not be more than two-thirds full. For foods such as rice and beans (which tend to foam), do not fill the pot more than half-full.

4 To close and lock the lid, grab the handle and rotate the lid clockwise about 10 degrees until the ▼ mark on the lid lines up with the ▲ mark on the cooker base. A chime will sound when the lid is locked. Turn the pressure release valve to the correct setting—open or closed—for your recipe.

5 Choose the desired cooking function and program the cooker. Adjust pressure,

temperature and cook times according to the directions in your recipe, if necessary.

6 When the dish is done, release the pressure and steam that have built up during cooking. This can be done in one of two ways, depending on what type of food you are cooking:

QUICK RELEASE Turn the pressure release valve to the open or venting position to speedily release steam until the float valve drops down. Using the quick release prevents pasta, vegetables, grains and more delicate meat, poultry and fish from becoming overcooked and mushy.

NATURAL RELEASE Leave the pressure release valve in the closed position. The cooker will begin to cool down and the float valve will drop down on its own. This can take 10 to 15 minutes or even longer. It allows heartier foods such as large roasts to continue cooking in the residual heat.

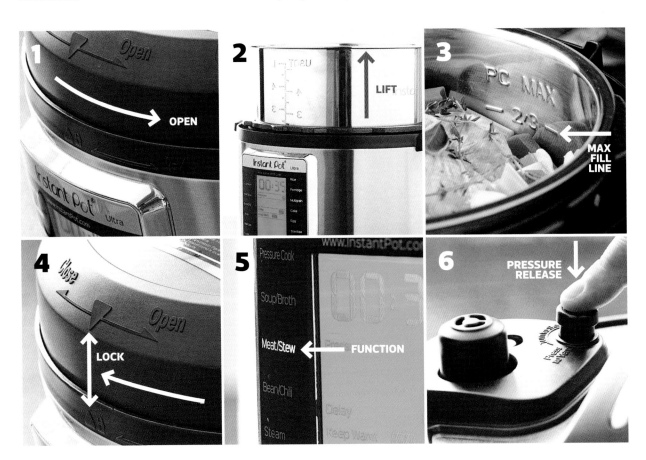

Instant Pots take the place of several kitchen appliances, saving you space and time.

BREAKFAST

WHETHER YOU LIKE TO START THE DAY
WITH A SWEET BITE OR YOU PREFER A MORE
SAVORY OPTION, THERE'S SOMETHING
DELICIOUS TO MAKE IN YOUR INSTANT POT
EVERY MORNING.

Southwestern
Breakfast Bowl,
page 16

**Stone-Ground Grits
With Toppings**

Stone-Ground Grits With Toppings

Cheesy grits make for a tasty and filling breakfast; they're also yummy as a side dish with grilled pork chops or steak for dinner.

START TO FINISH 25 minutes
(10 minutes active)

SERVINGS 6

INGREDIENTS

- ¼ cup butter
- 1 cup stone-ground grits
- 3 cups water
- 1 teaspoon salt
- 1½ cups milk
- 1 cup shredded cheddar cheese
  Garnishes: shredded cheddar cheese, snipped chives, crumbled bacon

1 On an Instant Pot, select Sauté; add butter and stir to melt. Add grits; stir.
2 Pour in water and salt.
3 Lock lid; set pressure release valve to Sealing. Select Pressure Cook. Select High Pressure; set timer for 10 minutes.
4 When time is up, use natural release for 10 minutes, then set pressure release valve to Venting to release remaining pressure. Unlock lid.
5 Stir in milk and shredded cheese until melted.
6 Serve with desired toppings.

Steel-Cut Oats With Spiced Apples

Steel-cut oats are high in protein and have more fiber than rolled.

START TO FINISH 10 minutes
(5 minutes active)

SERVINGS 4

Steel-Cut
Oats With
Spiced Apples

INGREDIENTS

- 2 tablespoons butter
- 1 cup steel-cut oats
- 2½ cups water
- 3 tablespoons brown sugar
- 2 teaspoons cinnamon, divided
- 1 small Granny Smith apple, diced
- 1 small Honeycrisp apple, diced
- ½ teaspoon nutmeg

1 On an Instant Pot, select Sauté; add butter and stir to melt.
2 Add oats and stir to coat with butter for 2 minutes.
3 Pour in water, brown sugar and 1 teaspoon cinnamon. Stir to combine.
4 Lock lid; set pressure release valve to Sealing. Select Pressure Cook; set timer for 5 minutes.
5 When time is up, use natural release for 5 minutes, then set pressure release valve to Venting to release remaining pressure. Unlock lid.
6 Combine diced apples in a medium bowl with remaining cinnamon and nutmeg.
7 Serve oatmeal with diced spiced apple mixture on top.

Double Apple Multigrain Porridge

Double Apple Multigrain Porridge

High-fiber multigrain cereal will keep you satiated for hours.

START TO FINISH 30 minutes
(5 minutes active)

SERVINGS 4

INGREDIENTS

- Nonstick cooking spray
- 1 cup multigrain cereal (such as Bob's Red Mill 8-Grain Hot Cereal)
- 1 cup applesauce
- ¼ cup chopped dried apples
- 1 tablespoon brown sugar
- 2 cups cold water
- ⅛ teaspoon salt
  Garnishes: butter, half-and-half, ground cinnamon

1 Spray Instant Pot lightly with cooking spray. Add cereal, applesauce, dried apples, brown sugar, water and salt to pot. Stir well.

2 Lock lid; set pressure release valve to Sealing. Select Pressure Cook; set timer for 15 minutes.

3 When time is up, use natural release. Unlock lid. Stir porridge well, allowing any excess liquid to be absorbed.

4 To serve, divide among four bowls. Top each with a pat of butter and a little bit of half-and-half. Sprinkle with cinnamon. Serve immediately.

Southwestern Breakfast Bowl

Serve all the extras on the side so everyone can make their bowl to taste.

START TO FINISH 25 minutes
(10 minutes active)

SERVINGS 4

INGREDIENTS

- 6 large eggs
- 3 tablespoons melted butter
- 1 teaspoon kosher salt
- ¼ teaspoon ground black pepper
- ½ pound cooked sausage, crumbled
- ½ cup shredded cheddar cheese
- ½ cup salsa
- ½ cup sour cream
- 1 avocado, cubed
- ¼ cup chopped scallions
  Garnishes: sliced jalapeño, cilantro sprigs

1 In a large bowl, mix eggs, butter, salt and pepper.

2 On an Instant Pot, select Sauté; add egg mixture to pot. Cook for 4 to 5 minutes while gently stirring with rubber spatula. When eggs begin to firm up, add cooked sausage and cheese and continue to cook until eggs are fully cooked. Select Cancel.

3 To serve, divide eggs between four bowls; top evenly with salsa, sour cream, avocado and scallions (or serve toppings on the side). Garnish, as desired.

Sausage Gravy Over Biscuits

Use your favorite biscuit recipe for this classic Southern dish. We doubt you'll have leftover gravy—but if you do, serve it over mashed potatoes.

START TO FINISH 15 minutes
(10 minutes active)

SERVINGS 6

INGREDIENTS

Vegetable cooking spray
1 (6-ounce) tube ground mild pork sausage
½ cup chicken broth
½ cup flour
1½ cups milk
1½ cups half-and-half
1 teaspoon salt
½ teaspoon black pepper
Freshly baked hot biscuits

Garnishes: cracked pepper, chopped parsley

1 Spray inner pot of Instant Pot with vegetable cooking spray. Select Sauté; crumble sausage and add to pot; cook for 3 minutes, stirring constantly.
2 Pour in broth.
3 Lock lid; set pressure release valve to Sealing. Select Pressure Cook; set timer for 5 minutes.
4 When time is up, use natural release for 5 minutes, then release remaining pressure. Unlock lid.
5 In a medium bowl, whisk together flour, milk, half-and-half, salt and black pepper.
6 Press Sauté and stir in milk mixture, whisking until thickened.
7 Serve over hot biscuits and garnish with cracked pepper and chopped parsley.

Blueberry
Breakfast
Casserole

Blueberry Breakfast Casserole

If bread pudding for breakfast is your idea of yum, this dish is for you!

START TO FINISH 30 minutes
(5 minutes active)

SERVINGS 4

INGREDIENTS

- 1 cup whole milk
- 2 large eggs
- ¼ cup brown sugar
- ½ teaspoon almond extract
- ½ teaspoon cinnamon
- 1 cup fresh blueberries
- 4 thick slices French bread cut into 2-inch pieces
  Vegetable cooking spray
  Garnish: powdered sugar

1 In a large bowl, whisk together milk, eggs, brown sugar, almond extract and cinnamon until well blended. Gently fold in blueberries and bread pieces until well coated.

2 Spray baking dish that fits in pot with cooking spray; pour bread mixture into dish.

3 Place steam rack in Instant Pot; pour in ¾ cup water. Place baking dish on rack.

4 Lock lid; set pressure release valve to Sealing. Select Pressure Cook; set timer for 25 minutes.

5 When time is up, unlock lid; carefully remove dish from pot. Sprinkle with powdered sugar to serve.

Huevos Rancheros

If you can't find tostada shells, just fry corn tortillas in a little oil for about 30 seconds per side. Drain on paper towels and keep them warm until you're ready to assemble the dish.

START TO FINISH 15 minutes
(10 minutes active)

SERVINGS 4

INGREDIENTS

- 1 (14.5-ounce) can fire-roasted diced tomatoes, undrained

Hard-Boiled Eggs

- 1 (15-ounce) can black beans, undrained
- 1 cubanelle pepper, seeded and chopped
- ½ cup frozen roasted corn
- ¼ teaspoon ground cumin
- 4 poached eggs (or however you like them cooked)
- 8 tostada shells, warmed
- ¼ cup sliced scallions
- ¾ cup shredded Mexican-style four-cheese blend
- ¼ cup chopped fresh cilantro
  Garnish: hot sauce

1 In an Instant Pot, stir together tomatoes, black beans, pepper, corn and cumin.

2 Lock lid; set pressure release valve to Sealing. Select Pressure Cook. Select High Pressure; set timer for 5 minutes.

3 When time is up, use quick release.

4 Open lid; carefully nestle eggs in bean mixture. Cover pot; let stand 1 minute or until eggs are just warm.

5 Place 2 warmed tostada shells, overlapping slightly, on each of 4 serving plates. Spoon ¾ cup bean mixture down centers of shells on each plate. Sprinkle each with 1 tablespoon scallions.

6 Top each with an egg; sprinkle evenly with cheese and cilantro. Serve immediately with hot sauce on the side, if desired.

Hard-Boiled Eggs

Hard-boiled eggs are good to have on hand for snacking, sliced to add to salads or making deviled eggs. The Instant Pot cooks them perfectly!

START TO FINISH 15 minutes
(5 minutes active)

SERVINGS 6

INGREDIENTS

- 6 large eggs
  Bowl of ice
  Salt and pepper

1 Place steamer rack in bottom of Instant Pot. Add eggs to rack. Pour 1 cup of water into pot.

2 Lock lid; set pressure release valve to Sealing. Select Pressure Cook; set timer for 5 minutes.

3 When time is up, use natural release for 5 minutes, then quick-release remaining pressure. Unlock lid.

4 Remove eggs; place in a bowl of ice.

5 Peel eggs; sprinkle with salt and pepper to taste.

QUICK TIP

Older eggs are easier to peel. Supermarket eggs are likely old enough. Eggs from the farmers market should sit a week.

Florentine Frittata

Eggs, spinach and bacon combine in this easy but impressive-looking dish that also makes a tasty lunch when served with some mixed greens.

START TO FINISH 25 minutes
(5 minutes active)

SERVINGS 6

INGREDIENTS

- 5 large eggs
- 2 tablespoons whole milk
- 1 teaspoon mustard powder
- 1 teaspoon kosher salt
- 1/2 teaspoon ground black pepper
- 1 cup fresh spinach, chopped
- 6 slices bacon, chopped
- 2 cups frozen shredded hash brown potatoes, thawed
- 2 tablespoons olive oil

1 In a medium bowl, whisk together eggs, milk, mustard powder, salt, pepper and spinach; set aside.

2 On an Instant Pot, select Sauté. Add bacon to pot; cook until crisp. Using a slotted spoon, remove bacon to a paper towel–lined plate.

3 Add hash browns in an even layer and brown, without stirring, 6 to 8 minutes. Drizzle with oil; turn hash browns in sections. Cook without stirring an additional 4 to 6 minutes or until browned.

4 Select Cancel to turn off pot. Remove hash browns to a plate, leaving any remaining drippings in pot.

5 Pour egg mixture into pot; use a wooden spoon to scrape brown bits from bottom of pot.

6 Return hash browns to pot and fold in gently; sprinkle bacon evenly over top. Lock lid; set pressure release valve to Sealing.

7 Select Pressure Cook. Select Low Pressure; set timer for 1 minute.

8 When time is up, use quick release. Unlock lid; cut frittata into wedges and serve warm.

Sausage Breakfast Casserole

Start a cold day off right with this hearty, cheesy casserole. If you've got leftovers, wrap them tightly and store for up to 1 month in the freezer.

START TO FINISH 30 minutes
(15 minutes active)

SERVINGS 8

INGREDIENTS

- 1 (16-ounce) tube mild sausage
- 1/2 teaspoon salt
- 1/4 teaspoon ground black pepper
- 1/3 cup chopped onion
- 8 large eggs
- 1/2 cup milk
- 8 slices white bread, torn into chunks
- 1 cup shredded cheddar cheese
  Chopped parsley

1 On an Instant Pot, select Sauté. Crumble sausage and add to pot. Cook until no longer pink, about 5 minutes.

2 Add salt, pepper and onion; cook for 3 minutes.

3 Remove mixture and set aside.

4 Spray 7-inch square pan with vegetable cooking spray.

5 In a medium bowl, whisk together eggs and milk. Fold in bread. Stir in meat mixture.

6 Pour into prepared pan. Top with shredded cheese.

7 Place steam rack in bottom of Instant Pot and pour 1 cup of water in pot. Place pan on rack.

8 Lock lid; set pressure release valve to Sealing. Select Pressure Cook. Select High Pressure; set timer for 12 minutes.

9 When time is up, use natural release for 10 minutes, then set pressure release valve to Venting to release remaining pressure. Unlock lid.

10 Carefully remove pan from Instant Pot and sprinkle with parsley.

Seeded Oatmeal With Apricots

Chia seeds and flaxseeds are both superfoods packed with fiber, antioxidants and healthy fats.

START TO FINISH 25 minutes

(5 minutes active)

SERVINGS 4

INGREDIENTS

Nonstick cooking spray
2¼ cups water
1 cup unsweetened plain or vanilla almond, soy, or cashew milk
Pinch of salt
½ teaspoon chia seeds
1 teaspoon flaxseeds
¼ cup chopped dried apricots
1 cup old-fashioned oats
1 teaspoon pumpkin pie spice
Maple syrup
¼ cup chopped toasted pecans or walnuts

1 Spray inner pot of Instant Pot lightly with cooking spray. In the Instant Pot, stir water and milk. Add salt, chia seeds, flaxseeds, apricots and oats.

2 Lock lid; set pressure release valve to Sealing. Select Pressure Cook. Select High Pressure; set timer for 10 minutes.

3 When time is up, use natural release. Unlock lid.

4 If mixture seems watery, place the lid back on and let sit for an additional 5 minutes. Stir in pumpkin pie spice and maple syrup to taste. Top each bowl with toasted nuts.

Breakfast Quinoa With Fruit

Simple, elegant and healthy—make this dish the centerpiece of a good-for-you brunch with friends. Use agave instead of honey to make it vegan.

START TO FINISH 25 minutes
(10 minutes active)

SERVINGS 4

INGREDIENTS

1 cup tricolor quinoa, rinsed
3 cups vanilla almond milk, divided
¼ teaspoon kosher salt
¼ teaspoon ground cinnamon
¼ teaspoon ground nutmeg
1 cup blueberries
1 cup sliced nectarine
1 cup sliced strawberries
¼ cup slivered almonds
Honey or agave

1 In an Instant Pot, add quinoa, 2 cups almond milk, salt, cinnamon and nutmeg.

2 Lock lid; set pressure release valve to Sealing. Select Pressure Cook. Select High Pressure; set timer for 2 minutes.

3 When time is up, use natural release for 12 minutes, then set pressure release valve to Venting to release remaining pressure.

4 Unlock lid; use fork to fluff quinoa.

5 To serve, divide the quinoa evenly among four bowls. Pour ¼ cup of vanilla almond milk over each serving. Top with fruit and almonds; drizzle with honey or agave, and serve immediately.

Egg & Sausage Muffins

In a hurry? These will be on the table in minutes, or pack one for the office.

START TO FINISH 25 minutes
(5 minutes active)

SERVINGS 4

INGREDIENTS

- 3 teaspoons olive oil, divided
- 1/2 cup cooked sausage, crumbled
- 4 small kale leaves, chopped
- 4 large eggs
- 1/4 cup heavy cream
- 1/2 teaspoon kosher salt
- 1/2 teaspoon ground black pepper
- 1/4 cup shredded cheddar cheese
- 1 cup water
  Garnish: chopped chives

1 Use 1 teaspoon olive oil to grease the bottom and insides of 4 silicone muffin cups.

2 On an Instant Pot, select Sauté; pour in remaining olive oil. Add sausage; cook for 2 minutes. Add kale; cook until kale is wilted, 2 to 3 minutes longer.

3 Meanwhile, in a medium bowl, lightly beat eggs, cream, salt and pepper.

4 Select Cancel. Divide kale-sausage mixture among the four muffin cups. Pour egg mixture evenly over kale and sausage; stir lightly with fork. Top each with 1 tablespoon cheese. Loosely cover cups with foil.

5 Pour 1 cup water into Instant Pot. Place steam rack inside. Place muffin cups on rack.

6 Lock lid; set pressure release valve to Sealing. Select Pressure Cook; set timer for 5 minutes.

7 When time is up, use natural release for 10 minutes, then set pressure release valve to Venting to release remaining pressure. Unlock lid; remove muffins from pot. Serve warm and garnish with chives, if desired.

Shakshuka

This Middle Eastern favorite has become increasingly popular worldwide as a hearty dish for any time of day.

Shakshuka

START TO FINISH 25 minutes
(10 minutes active)

SERVINGS 4

INGREDIENTS

- 2 tablespoons olive oil
- 1 red bell pepper, chopped
- 1 onion, chopped
- 3 cloves garlic, minced
- 2 teaspoons sugar
- 2 teaspoons ground cumin
- 1 teaspoon paprika
- 1 teaspoon chili powder
- 1/2 teaspoon kosher salt
- 1/4 teaspoon red pepper flakes
- 1 (28-ounce) can crushed tomatoes
- 4 large eggs
- 3/4 cup crumbled feta cheese
  Garnishes: chopped parsley, parsley leaves

1 In an Instant Pot, add oil. Select Sauté. Add bell pepper and onion; cook and stir 3 minutes. Add garlic, sugar, cumin, paprika, chili powder, salt and red pepper flakes; cook and stir 1 minute. Stir in tomatoes; mix well.

2 Lock lid; set pressure release valve to Sealing. Select Pressure Cook. Select High Pressure; set timer for 10 minutes.

3 When time is up, select cancel; use quick release. Unlock lid. Make 4 wells in sauce for eggs, leaving space between each. Crack each egg into a well.

4 Lock lid; set pressure release valve to Sealing. Select Manual. Select Low Pressure; set timer for 1 minute.

5 When time is up, select Cancel; use quick release. Place on serving dish; sprinkle with feta cheese and garnish, as desired.

French Toast Bake

Select High Pressure; set timer for
for 20 minutes. When time is up, use
natural release. Unlock lid.
4 Carefully remove dish and let cool
for 10 minutes before serving. Top with
powdered sugar and maple syrup.

Avocado Toast With Hard-Boiled Eggs

Kick-start your morning with a
colorful, protein-packed breakfast.
START TO FINISH 35 minutes
(13 minutes active)
SERVINGS 4

INGREDIENTS
4   large raw eggs
2   avocados, pitted and peeled
½   jalapeño, seeded and finely
      diced
3   tablespoons lemon juice
1   teaspoon Dijon mustard
¼   teaspoon kosher salt
4   slices multigrain or whole-
      wheat bread, toasted
½   cup halved grape tomatoes
2   tablespoons minced red onion
1   watermelon radish, sliced
      Garnish: cilantro sprigs

1 Place steamer basket in Instant Pot.
Pour in 1 cup water. Place eggs
in basket.
2 Lock lid; set pressure release valve
to Sealing. Select Pressure Cook; set
timer for 7 minutes.
3 Meanwhile, in a medium bowl,
place 2 cups water and 2 cups ice
cubes; set aside.
4 In another bowl, mash avocado,
jalapeño, lemon juice, mustard and
salt; set aside.
5 When time is up, use quick release.
Unlock lid; place eggs in ice water for
3 minutes.
6 Peel eggs; cut in half. Crumble
2 yolks (use remaining yolks in
another dish) and slice whites.
7 Spread avocado mixture on bread
slices. Sprinkle with crumbled yolks,
sliced whites, tomatoes, onion and
radish. Garnish with cilantro sprigs.

French Toast Bake

Cinnamon swirl bread makes
this brunch favorite a cinch
to serve.
START TO FINISH 45 minutes
(15 minutes active)
SERVINGS 4

INGREDIENTS
      Nonstick cooking spray
6   eggs
¾   cup half-and-half or light cream
1   teaspoon vanilla extract
½   teaspoon ground nutmeg
1   tablespoon pure maple syrup
2   thick slices cinnamon swirl
      bread, cubed
      Powdered sugar
      Maple syrup, for drizzling

1 Place a steam rack in Instant
Pot. Pour in 1½ cups water. Spray a
1-quart soufflé dish with nonstick
cooking spray.
2 In a medium bowl, whisk together
eggs, half-and-half, vanilla, nutmeg
and maple syrup. Gently stir in
bread. Pour mixture into prepared
dish. Cover dish with foil; place on
steam rack.
3 Lock lid; set pressure release valve
to Sealing. Select Pressure Cook.

QUICK TIP

Use a potato masher to mash your avocados; be sure to leave some chunkier pieces for Instagrammable results.

Avocado Toast With Hard-Boiled Eggs

25

APPETIZERS & BEVERAGES

TRY THESE CLASSICS-
WITH-A-TWIST (INCLUDING
MOUTHWATERING DIPS
AND FESTIVE DRINKS)
FOR YOUR NEXT GATHERING
OR SPECIAL MEAL.

Supreme Pizza Dip, page 32

Crab Rangoon Dip

cream cheese, mozzarella cheese, mayonnaise, sweet and sour sauce, Worcestershire sauce, soy sauce and most of the scallions (set aside a few green slices for garnish). Gently stir in crabmeat.

3 Place bowl on rack in pot. Lock lid; set pressure release valve to Sealing. Select Pressure Cook. Select Low Pressure; set timer for 8 minutes.

4 When time is up, use quick release. Unlock lid.

5 Carefully remove dish and sprinkle with remaining scallion slices. Serve with pita chips.

Spicy Jalapeño Salsa

This is so much better than supermarket versions! Use more or fewer peppers to suit your taste.

START TO FINISH 10 minutes
(5 minutes active)

SERVINGS 8

INGREDIENTS

- 8 large tomatoes, chopped
- 4 cloves garlic, minced
- 3 jalapeño peppers, diced
- 1 red bell pepper, diced
- 1 red onion, chopped
- 1 white onion, chopped
- 1 tablespoon cumin
- 2 teaspoons salt
- 1 teaspoon ground black pepper
- ¹/₂ teaspoon baking soda
- 3 tablespoons tomato paste
- 1 tablespoon fresh lime juice
- 1 tablespoon red wine vinegar
- ¹/₄ cup chopped cilantro
  Garnish: cilantro leaves

1 Add tomatoes, garlic, peppers, onions, cumin, salt, black pepper and baking soda to Instant Pot.

2 Lock lid; set pressure release valve to Sealing. Select Pressure Cook. Select High Pressure; set timer for 5 minutes.

3 When time is up, use natural release for 10 minutes, then quick-release remaining pressure.

4 Unlock lid. Stir in tomato paste, lime juice, vinegar and cilantro.

5 Let cool completely before serving. Garnish with cilantro.

Crab Rangoon Dip

This creamy dip is based on the popular fried-wonton appetizer.

START TO FINISH 30 minutes
(15 minutes active)

SERVINGS 12 to 16

INGREDIENTS

- 1 (8-ounce) package cream cheese, cut into cubes
- 1 cup finely shredded mozzarella cheese
- ¹/₂ cup mayonnaise
- ¹/₃ cup sweet and sour sauce
- 1 teaspoon Worcestershire sauce
- ¹/₂ teaspoon soy sauce
- 2 scallions, thinly sliced (white and green parts)
- 2 (6-ounce) cans lump crabmeat, drained, flaked, and cartilage removed
  Pita chips

1 Place steam rack in an Instant Pot. Add 1¹/₂ cups water to pot.

2 In a 3- to 4-cup glass bowl, mix

Chili Con Queso Dip

This cheesy dip is best served warm.

START TO FINISH 30 minutes
(10 minutes active)

SERVINGS 20

INGREDIENTS

- 2 tablespoons butter
- 1 cup diced onion
- 1 teaspoon minced garlic
- 2 (4-ounce) cans chopped green chiles
- 1 tablespoon chili powder
- 1 teaspoon cumin
- 3 tablespoons flour
- 2 cups milk
- 2 cups grated pepper Jack cheese
- 2 cups grated white cheddar cheese
- ½ (8-ounce) package cream cheese
- 1 teaspoon salt
- ½ teaspoon ground black pepper

Garnishes: sliced scallions, chopped tomato, sliced jalapeños, cilantro leaves, corn kernels

Tortilla chips

1 Press Sauté; melt butter in Instant Pot. Add onion and garlic and cook for 3 minutes.

2 Add in chopped green chiles, chili powder, cumin and flour. Cook for 1 minute, then whisk in milk.

3 Bring to a boil. Press Stop. Stir in cheeses until they melt; add salt and pepper.

4 Cover for 3 minutes. Remove lid, garnish with desired toppings, and serve with tortilla chips on the side.

Barbecue Chicken Wings

Barbecue Chicken Wings

These tasty wings get a brown sugar and spice coat first, then an additional coat of barbecue sauce for another layer of flavor.

START TO FINISH 25 minutes
(15 minutes active)

SERVINGS 4

INGREDIENTS

- 3 tablespoons light brown sugar
- 1 teaspoon salt
- ½ teaspoon cayenne pepper
- ½ teaspoon garlic powder
- ½ teaspoon ground black pepper
- 3 pounds chicken wings and drumettes
- 1 cup barbecue sauce
- 3 tablespoons hot sauce
  Garnishes: blue cheese dressing, ranch dressing, celery sticks, carrot sticks

1 Place the steam rack in the bottom of Instant Pot. Pour in 1 cup of water.
2 Combine brown sugar and next 4 ingredients in a large bowl. Toss chicken in mixture to coat.
3 Arrange chicken on top of rack.
4 Lock lid; set pressure release valve to Sealing. Select Pressure Cook. Select High Pressure; set timer for 5 minutes.
5 When time is up, use natural release for 10 minutes, then quick-release remaining pressure. Remove lid.
6 Take wings out of Instant Pot; toss in mixture of barbecue and hot sauces.
7 Place wings on baking sheet and place under the broiler for 2-3 minutes or until crispy. Serve with garnishes on the side.

Buffalo Chicken Wings

Finish these wings under the broiler for a couple of minutes for extra crispness. Don't forget the blue cheese (or ranch) dressing on the side for dipping!

START TO FINISH 20 minutes
(5 minutes active)

SERVINGS 4

Hawaiian Meatballs With Pineapple Glaze

INGREDIENTS

- 1 tablespoon seasoned salt
- 1 tablespoon paprika
- 1 teaspoon ground black pepper
- 3 pounds chicken wings and drumettes
- 1 cup hot sauce
- 1 tablespoon honey
- 1 teaspoon garlic powder
- 3 tablespoons melted butter

1 In a large bowl, combine seasoned salt, paprika and black pepper. Add wings and drumettes; toss to coat.
2 Pour 1 cup of water into inner pot. Place steam rack inside Instant Pot. Place wings on rack.
3 Lock lid; set pressure release valve to Sealing. Select Pressure Cook. Select High Pressure; set timer for 10 minutes.
4 When time is up, use natural release for 5 minutes, then quick-release remaining pressure. Unlock lid.
5 Place wings in a large bowl.
6 In a small bowl, mix hot sauce, honey, garlic powder and butter. Pour half the sauce over wings and toss.
7 Line a baking sheet with foil; place a wire rack on top. Place wings on rack. Broil for 2 to 3 minutes per side or until crispy.
8 Brush wings with remaining sauce and serve.

Hawaiian Meatballs With Pineapple Glaze

These are always a hit at parties—consider doubling the batch! You can also sub in precooked turkey or vegetarian meatballs if you'd like.

START TO FINISH 30 minutes
(5 minutes active)

SERVINGS 6

INGREDIENTS

- 1 (32-ounce) bag precooked frozen meatballs
- 1 (14-ounce) can pineapple tidbits in juice, undrained
- ¾ cup brown sugar
- 2 tablespoons soy sauce
- 1 tablespoon cornstarch
  Garnish: cilantro leaves

1 Place meatballs in bottom of Instant Pot. Top with undrained pineapple bits, brown sugar and soy sauce.
2 Lock lid; set pressure release valve to Sealing. Select Pressure Cook. Select High Pressure; set timer for 7 minutes.
3 When time is up, use natural release for 5 minutes, then quick-release remaining pressure. Unlock lid.
4 Press Sauté, whisk in cornstarch and cook 1 minute or until thick.
5 Remove from pot; garnish with cilantro leaves and serve immediately.

Cocktail Maple Smokies

Old-school cool! These little smoked sausages have been a party favorite for years, but we switched things up by upgrading the sauce to barbecue and brown sugar with a hint of maple that complements the smoky goodness.

START TO FINISH 5 minutes
(2 minutes active)
SERVINGS 8

INGREDIENTS

- 2 (12-ounce) packages smoky cocktail sausages
- 1 cup barbecue sauce
- ¼ cup brown sugar
- 2 tablespoons white vinegar
- 1 tablespoon maple syrup
- ¼ cup chicken broth

1 Place all ingredients in Instant Pot, stirring to combine.
2 Lock lid; set pressure release valve to Sealing. Select Pressure Cook. Select High Pressure; set timer for 1 minute.
3 When time is up, use natural release for 5 minutes. Unlock lid.
4 Remove from pot and serve warm.

Chicken & Jalapeño Popper Dip

Panko breadcrumbs are larger and flatter than regular crumbs, giving the top of this dip an irresistible crunch.

START TO FINISH 15 minutes
(5 minutes active)
SERVINGS 10

INGREDIENTS

- 2 boneless, skinless chicken breasts
- 1 (8-ounce) package cream cheese
- 3 large jalapeños, sliced
- ½ cup chicken broth
- 8 ounces shredded cheddar cheese, divided
- 1 cup sour cream
- ⅓ cup panko breadcrumbs

1 In an Instant Pot, add chicken, cream cheese, jalapeños and broth.
2 Lock lid; set pressure release valve to Sealing. Select Pressure Cook. Select High Pressure; set timer for 12 minutes.
3 When time is up, use natural release for 10 minutes, then quick-release remaining pressure. Unlock lid.
4 Remove chicken and shred. Return to pot; add ¾ cup cheese and sour cream.
5 Place mixture in baking dish; top with remaining cheese and breadcrumbs.
6 Broil 2 minutes and serve with assorted crackers.

Deviled Eggs

Serve all of the garnishes on the side so your guests can load up their eggs the way they like them.

START TO FINISH 20 minutes
(10 minutes active)
SERVINGS 6

INGREDIENTS

- 6 large eggs
- 3 tablespoons mayonnaise
- 1 tablespoon olive oil
- 2 teaspoons mustard
- 1 teaspoon seafood seasoning
- ½ teaspoon ground black pepper
  Garnishes: sliced scallions, chives, caviar, cooked crumbled bacon, jalapeño slices

1 In an Instant Pot, place steam rack. Pour in 1 cup water. Place eggs on rack.
2 Lock lid; set pressure release valve to Sealing. Select Pressure Cook. Select High Pressure; set timer for 8 minutes.
3 When time is up, use quick release. Unlock lid.
4 Let eggs cool, then peel eggs; place in a bowl of cold water to chill.
5 Cut eggs in half lengthwise, remove yolks, and place in a small bowl. Add mayonnaise, olive oil and mustard; mash until very smooth. Season with the seafood seasoning and pepper.
6 Fill egg whites with yolk mixture; top with desired garnishes.

MORE TIME BUT WORTH IT

Supreme Pizza Dip

A bowl of delicious pizza toppings (including three types of meat!) to dip breadsticks into? Sign us up!

START TO FINISH 35 minutes
(10 minutes active)
SERVINGS 8

INGREDIENTS

- 1 (8-ounce) package cream cheese, cubed and softened
- 8 ounces shredded mozzarella cheese
- 1 small green bell pepper, chopped
- 1 small onion, chopped
- 4 slices cooked bacon, chopped
- ½ cup cooked sausage
- 12 pepperoni slices
  Garnishes: chopped parsley, red pepper flakes
  Breadsticks and crostini

1 Place steam rack in bottom of Instant Pot. Pour in 1 cup of water.
2 Grease a 1¾-quart round baking dish. In a large bowl, mix cream cheese, mozzarella, green pepper, onion, bacon and sausage. Place mixture in dish. Top with pepperoni slices. Cover tightly with foil.
3 Place on rack in Instant Pot.
4 Lock lid; set pressure release valve to Sealing. Press Pressure Cook. Select High Pressure; set timer for 15 minutes.
5 When time is up, use natural release for 5 minutes, then quick-release remaining pressure. Unlock lid and remove dish.
6 Garnish with parsley and red pepper flakes. Serve immediately with breadsticks and crostini.

QUICK TIP

Pile on the toppings with this tasty dip! Some we love: sliced black olives, a sprinkle of Parmesan, fresh basil leaves.

Cocktail Maple
Smokies

QUICK TIP

Other wine options for red sangria are rioja and syrah; if you'd like a white sangria, opt for sauvignon blanc or pinot grigio.

Hot Mulled
Sangria

Hot Buttered Rum

Hot Mulled Sangria

This winter warmer, full of aromatic spices, is perfect for parties or just when you want to gather by the fire.

START TO FINISH 20 minutes
(5 minutes active)
SERVINGS 12

INGREDIENTS

2   (750ml) bottles chianti
4   cinnamon sticks
1   tablespoon whole cloves
1   teaspoon juniper berries
2   star anise
1   cup sugar
1   apple, sliced
1   blood orange, sliced
1   navel orange, sliced
1   lime, sliced
    Garnishes: additional slices of apples, oranges and limes

1 Add all ingredients to Instant Pot.
2 Lock lid; set pressure release valve to Sealing. Select Pressure Cook. Select High Pressure; set timer for 1 minute.
3 When time is up, use Natural Release for 5 minutes, then quick-release remaining pressure. Remove lid. Strain mixture.
4 Garnish, as desired; serve immediately.

Hot Buttered Rum

Let this drink cool to room temperature and add a scoop of vanilla ice cream to transform it into a delicious summertime dessert.

START TO FINISH 6 minutes
(5 minutes active)
SERVINGS 4

INGREDIENTS

$^1/_2$ pound butter
$^1/_2$ cup brown sugar
2   cinnamon sticks, divided
$^1/_2$ teaspoon grated nutmeg
$^1/_8$ teaspoon kosher salt
1   cup spiced rum
    Garnish: cinnamon sticks

1 In an Instant Pot, add butter, brown sugar, cinnamon sticks, nutmeg and salt. Add 2 cups water; stir. Lock lid; set pressure release valve to Sealing. Select Pressure Cook. Select High Pressure; set timer for 1 minute.
2 Use natural release for 5 minutes, then release remaining pressure. Unlock lid.
3 Stir in rum. Ladle into glasses or mugs; garnish with cinnamon sticks.

Hot Mulled
Fruit Punch

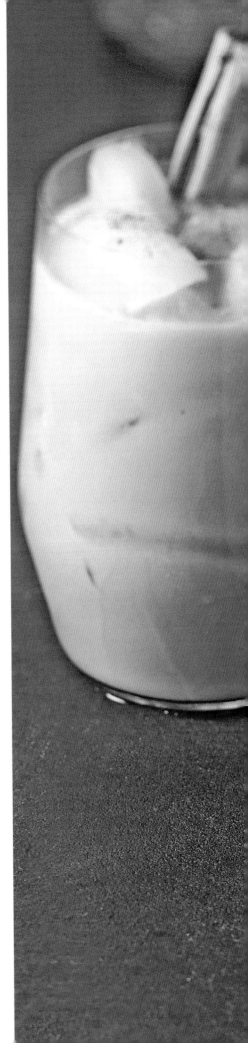

Hot Mulled
Fruit Punch

A simple but flavorful punch is a
great way to start any gathering.

START TO FINISH 15 minutes
(5 minutes active)

SERVINGS 12

INGREDIENTS

1 (48-ounce) bottle cranberry
juice
4 cinnamon sticks
1 tablespoon whole cloves
1 teaspoon juniper berries
2 star anise
1 cup granulated sugar
Garnishes: sliced apples, limes,
oranges

1 In an Instant Pot, stir together all
ingredients. Lock lid; set pressure
release valve to Sealing. Select
Pressure Cook. Select High Pressure;
set timer for 1 minute.
2 When time is up, use natural
release for 5 minutes, then release
remaining pressure. Unlock lid.
3 Strain and garnish, as desired.

Chai Tea Concentrate

Enjoy this warm or chilled, or try our adults-only White Russian boozy version!

START TO FINISH 15 minutes
(5 minutes active)
SERVINGS 6 cups

INGREDIENTS

6	cups water
1	tablespoon chopped ginger
4	cinnamon sticks
8	cloves
8	peppercorns
8	allspice berries
8	cardamom pods
10	black tea bags

1 Add all ingredients to Instant Pot.

2 Lock lid; set pressure release valve to Sealing. Select Pressure Cook. Select High Pressure; set timer for 5 minutes.

3 When time is up, use natural release for 10 minutes, then quick-release remaining pressure. Remove lid.

4 Remove tea bags. Refrigerate with spices.

5 When ready to use, strain concentrate and serve over ice.

TO MAKE CHAI TEA WHITE RUSSIAN:

1	ounce chai tea concentrate
1	ounce Kahlúa
1	ounce vodka
1	ounce heavy cream
1	ounce simple syrup
1/8	teaspoon nutmeg
	Ice cubes
	Garnish: grated nutmeg

Combine chai tea concentrate and remaining ingredients. Serve over ice. Top with additional nutmeg.

Apple &
Pear Cider

Apple & Pear Cider

This lightly spiced drink will warm you up from the inside on a chilly night.

START TO FINISH 25 minutes (5 minutes active)

SERVINGS 8

INGREDIENTS

- 3 Honeycrisp apples, cored and sliced
- 3 ripe Bosc pears, cored and sliced
- 2 cinnamon sticks
- 4 cardamom pods
- 1 tablespoon brown sugar
- 6 cups water
   Garnish: cinnamon sticks

1 In an Instant Pot, add apples, pears, cinnamon sticks, cardamom and sugar. Pour in water; stir.
2 Lock lid; set pressure release valve to Sealing. Select Pressure Cook. Select High Pressure; set timer for 10 minutes.
3 When time is up, use natural release. Pour mixture through a sieve.
4 Serve warm in heat-safe glasses; garnish each with a cinnamon stick.

Creamy Irish Coffee

This grown-up treat is perfect after dinner (use decaf if you're caffeine-sensitive).

START TO FINISH 10 minutes (5 minutes active)

SERVINGS 1

INGREDIENTS

- 2 teaspoons maple syrup
- 1 teaspoon brown sugar
- 2 teaspoons instant espresso powder
- 1 cup water
- 3 tablespoons Irish whiskey
- 2 tablespoons heavy cream
   Garnishes: whipped cream, chopped dark chocolate espresso beans

1 In an Instant Pot, combine maple syrup, brown sugar, espresso powder and water. Lock lid; set pressure release valve to Sealing. Select

Creamy Irish Coffee

Pressure Cook. Select High Pressure; set timer for 5 minutes.
2 When time is up, use natural release. Unlock lid; stir in whiskey and cream. Pour into glass mugs; garnish, as desired.

Killer Hot Chocolate

Amazingly rich and decadent—and so easy! For a frozen treat, let cool, then mix in a blender with 3 cups of ice.

START TO FINISH 10 minutes (5 minutes active)

SERVINGS 4

INGREDIENTS

- 2 cups whole milk
- 2 cups heavy cream
- ½ cup granulated sugar
- ¼ cup cocoa powder
- 1 teaspoon vanilla extract
   Garnishes: marshmallows, whipped cream, chocolate shavings

1 In an Instant Pot, add milk, cream, sugar, cocoa powder and vanilla. Whisk until well combined. Lock lid; set pressure release valve to Sealing. Select Pressure Cook. Select High Pressure; set timer for 2 minutes.
2 When time is up, select Cancel. Use natural release for 5 minutes; quick-release remaining pressure. Unlock lid; stir.
3 Strain through a sieve and pour into mugs. Garnish, as desired.

MEAT

BEEF AND PORK ARE BOTH
COOKED TO PERFECTION WITH THESE
MOUTHWATERING RECIPES.

Pork Tenderloin
With Thyme Gravy,
page 49

30-Minute Spaghetti

breadcrumbs, ¼ cup grated Parmesan cheese, 2 tablespoons milk, 1 teaspoon dried Italian seasoning, 2 cloves minced garlic, ½ teaspoon salt and 1 teaspoon black pepper. Shape into 1½-inch balls. Omit Step 1. Combine sauce ingredients in pot. Gently stir in meatballs. Cook at high pressure for 7 minutes; use natural release.

Ginger Beef Stir-Fry Over Basmati Rice

Put down your phone! You can make this dish in less time than it takes to call and pick up takeout.

START TO FINISH 20 minutes
(10 minutes active)

SERVINGS 4

INGREDIENTS

- 1 tablespoon sesame oil
- 2 pounds sirloin steak, sliced into strips
- 1 onion, sliced
- 1 red bell pepper, sliced
- 1 green bell pepper, sliced
- 2 tablespoons minced ginger
- 1 teaspoon minced garlic
- 1 teaspoon Sriracha sauce
- ½ cup soy sauce
- ¼ cup rice wine vinegar
- 2 tablespoons honey
- 1 teaspoon Chinese five spice seasoning
- 2 cups beef broth
  Hot cooked basmati rice
  Garnish: sliced scallion

1 On an Instant Pot, select Sauté; heat oil. Add steak; cook 2 minutes. Remove.
2 Add onion, peppers, ginger and garlic; cook for 2 minutes.
3 Add Sriracha, soy sauce, rice wine vinegar, honey, seasoning and broth.
4 Lock lid; set pressure release valve to Sealing. Select Pressure Cook. Select High Pressure; set timer for 5 minutes.
5 When time is up, use natural release for 10 minutes, then quick-release remaining pressure. Unlock lid.
6 Serve with rice. Garnish, as desired.

30-Minute Spaghetti

This is perfect for nights when you want a crowd-pleasing meal in a flash.

START TO FINISH 30 minutes
(15 minutes active)

SERVINGS 6

INGREDIENTS

- 1 pound ground beef
- 2 cups sliced fresh mushrooms (6 ounces)
- ½ cup chopped onion (1 medium)
- 1 green bell pepper, chopped
- 2 cloves garlic, minced
- 1 teaspoon sugar
- 1 teaspoon dried oregano, crushed
- 2 bay leaves
- 1 (28-ounce) can stewed tomatoes
- 1 (6-ounce) can tomato paste
- ½ cup red wine
- 6 cups (12 ounces uncooked) hot cooked spaghetti
  Parmesan cheese, for serving

1 On an Instant Pot, select Sauté. Add beef; cook until browned. Drain fat.
2 Add mushrooms, onion, green pepper, garlic, sugar, oregano, bay leaves, tomatoes, tomato paste and wine to pot.
3 Lock lid; set pressure release valve to Sealing. Select Pressure Cook. Select High Pressure; set timer for 6 minutes.
4 When time is up, use quick release. Unlock lid.
5 Remove bay leaves. Top spaghetti with meat sauce and Parmesan cheese.
MEATBALL VARIATION Beat 1 egg in a medium bowl. Stir in ¼ cup dry

Teriyaki Beef Stir-Fry

If you don't have sirloin steak, substitute flank steak instead. Add broccoli or other veggies if you'd like.

START TO FINISH 20 minutes (10 minutes active)

SERVINGS 4

INGREDIENTS

- 1 tablespoon vegetable oil
- 1½ pounds sirloin steak, trimmed and sliced
- 1 small onion, sliced
- ¼ cup soy sauce
- ¼ cup brown sugar
- 1 tablespoon honey
- 1 teaspoon grated ginger
- 1 tablespoon minced garlic
- 3 tablespoons water
- 2 tablespoons cornstarch
- 1 cup snow peas, trimmed
  Hot cooked rice
  Garnishes: matchstick-cut raw carrots, red pepper flakes, sliced scallions

1 On an Instant Pot, select Sauté; heat oil. Add steak and onion and cook for 2 minutes.

2 Add soy sauce, brown sugar, honey, ginger and garlic and mix well.

3 Lock lid; set pressure release valve to Sealing. Select Pressure Cook. Select High Pressure; set timer for 5 minutes.

4 When time is up, use quick release. Unlock lid.

5 In a small bowl, whisk water and cornstarch together. Stir into beef mixture.

6 Add snow peas; press Sauté again and cook for 1 minute or until thickened.

7 Serve over hot cooked rice and garnish, as desired.

**Penne With
Meat Sauce**

Penne With Meat Sauce

Use a good-quality tomato sauce, or make your own for this dish.

START TO FINISH 25 minutes
(5 minutes active)
SERVINGS 4

INGREDIENTS

- 1 tablespoon olive oil
- 1 onion, chopped
- 1 teaspoon minced garlic
- 1 pound lean ground beef
- 1 teaspoon salt
- 1/2 teaspoon ground black pepper
- 1 (28-ounce) jar tomato-basil pasta sauce
- 2 cups water
- 8 ounces dry mezze penne pasta
  Freshly grated Parmesan cheese
  Garnish: basil or parsley leaves

1 On an Instant Pot, select Sauté; heat oil. Add onion; sauté for 3 minutes. Add garlic; cook 1 minute.
2 Add ground beef, salt and pepper and stir with a wooden spoon to break up meat for 3 minutes.
3 Add pasta sauce, water and dry pasta; stir.
4 Lock lid; set pressure release valve to Sealing. Select Pressure Cook. Select High Pressure; set timer for 8 minutes.
5 When time is up, use natural release for 10 minutes, then quick-release remaining pressure. Unlock lid.
6 Serve with grated Parmesan and garnish with basil or parsley leaves, as desired.

Flank Steak Fajitas

This restaurant favorite cooks up easily at home with an Instant Pot. Serve plenty of toppings on the side.

START TO FINISH 20 minutes
(5 minutes active)
SERVINGS 6

INGREDIENTS

- 1 1/2 pounds top round steak, sliced
- 1 tablespoon taco seasoning
- 3/4 cup beef broth
- 1 onion, sliced
- 1 green bell pepper, sliced
- 1 red bell pepper, sliced
- 1 tablespoon lime juice
  Tortillas
  Garnishes: sour cream, guacamole, salsa, cilantro leaves

1 In an Instant Pot, add steak; sprinkle with taco seasoning.
2 Pour broth over steak and add onion and bell pepper slices.
3 Lock lid; set pressure release valve to Sealing. Select Pressure Cook. Select High Pressure; set timer for 5 minutes.
4 When time is up, use natural release for 10 minutes, then quick-release remaining pressure. Unlock lid. Stir in lime juice.
5 Warm the tortillas; serve alongside meat and desired toppings.

Juicy Pork Chops Over Rice

These chops will be fork-tender, and the cooking juices and broth will form a sauce for the rice.

START TO FINISH 20 minutes
(10 minutes active)
SERVINGS 4

INGREDIENTS

- 1/4 cup brown sugar
- 1 teaspoon salt
- 1 teaspoon ground black pepper
- 1 teaspoon garlic powder
- 1 teaspoon paprika
- 4 (1-inch-thick) boneless pork chops
- 2 tablespoons butter
- 2 cups chicken broth
- 1 tablespoon Worcestershire sauce
  Hot cooked rice

1 In a small bowl, combine brown sugar, salt, pepper, garlic powder and paprika. Rub mixture on both sides of pork chops.
2 On an Instant Pot, select Sauté; heat butter. Add pork chops and cook 2 minutes per side. Remove chops and set aside. Press Cancel.
3 Add broth and Worcestershire sauce; stir with wooden spoon to deglaze the brown bits off the bottom.
4 Add chops back to pot; lock lid; set pressure release valve to Sealing. Select Pressure Cook. Select High Pressure; set timer for 7 minutes.
5 When time is up, use natural release for 10 minutes, then quick-release remaining pressure. Unlock lid.
6 Remove chops; let rest for 5 minutes. Serve over rice. Spoon some of the juices from the pot over the chops, and serve the rest on the side.

Mongolian Beef With Broccoli

This Chinese restaurant favorite is easier to make than you might think, and just as delicious!

START TO FINISH 25 minutes
(10 minutes active)
SERVINGS 6

INGREDIENTS

- 2 pounds beef flank steak, cut into strips
- 2 cups beef broth
- 1 teaspoon minced garlic
- 1/2 cup soy sauce
- 1 tablespoon honey
- 2 tablespoons sesame oil
- 2 tablespoons cornstarch
- 2 cups steamed broccoli florets
- 4 cups cooked white rice
  Garnishes: toasted sesame seeds, sliced scallions, red pepper flakes

1 In an Instant Pot, add steak.
2 In a large bowl, whisk together broth, garlic, soy sauce, honey and sesame oil. Pour into pot.
3 Lock lid; set pressure release valve to Sealing. Select Pressure Cook. Select High Pressure; set timer for 10 minutes.
4 When time is up, use quick release. Unlock lid.
5 Remove 1/4 cup of liquid to a small bowl; whisk in cornstarch. Add mixture back to Instant Pot and stir.
6 Stir broccoli into beef mixture. Serve over rice and garnish, as desired.

Orange Glazed Whole Ham

Make this honey-orange glazed ham the centerpiece of your holiday table.

START TO FINISH 28 minutes
(10 minutes active)

SERVINGS 12

INGREDIENTS

- 2 cups chicken broth
- 1 cup brown sugar
- 1 cup honey
- ¼ cup fresh orange juice
- 2 teaspoons orange zest
- 1 (4-pound) boneless spiral ham
  Garnishes: orange slices, bay leaves

1 Place a steam rack inside Instant Pot; pour in broth.
2 In a small bowl, combine brown sugar, honey, orange juice and zest. Brush over ham and in between slices. Place ham in Instant Pot.
3 Lock lid; set pressure release valve to Sealing. Select Pressure Cook. Select High Pressure; set timer for 8 minutes.
4 When time is up, use natural release for 10 minutes, then quick-release remaining pressure. Unlock lid.
5 Place ham on serving platter and garnish, as desired.

Philly Cheesesteak Subs

Freeze the steak for 20 minutes to make it easier to slice. Make it traditional with sautéed onions and some hot sauce, too.

START TO FINISH 30 minutes
(10 minutes active)

SERVINGS 4

INGREDIENTS

- 2 tablespoons butter
- 1 green bell pepper, sliced
- 1 red bell pepper, sliced
- 1 large yellow onion, sliced
- 2 pounds rib-eye steak, thinly sliced
- 2 tablespoons Worcestershire sauce
- 1 teaspoon salt
- 1 teaspoon ground black pepper
- 8 slices provolone cheese
- 4 hero or hoagie rolls

1 On an Instant Pot, select Sauté; heat butter. Add green and red peppers and onions and cook for 3 minutes. Add steak and Worcestershire sauce; stir to combine.
2 Lock lid; set pressure release valve to Sealing. Select Pressure Cook. Select high heat; set timer for 8 minutes.
3 When time is up, use natural release for 10 minutes, then quick-release remaining pressure. Unlock lid.
4 Divide steak mixture into four portions, place on rolls and top with cheese. Serve immediately.

Spaghetti & Meatballs

The spaghetti cooks together with the rest of the ingredients, so it absorbs the flavors from the meatballs and tomato sauce as it cooks. Serve this with Italian bread to soak up the sauce.

START TO FINISH 30 minutes
(5 minutes active)

SERVINGS 4

INGREDIENTS

- 1 pound frozen meatballs
- 1 (8-ounce) bag dry spaghetti or bucatini, broken in half
- 1 (28-ounce) jar tomato-basil pasta sauce
  Garnishes: grated Parmesan cheese, basil leaves

1 Place meatballs in bottom of Instant Pot. Sprinkle pasta on top.
2 Pour 3 cups water over pasta. Pour in pasta sauce.
3 Lock lid; set pressure release valve to Sealing. Select Pressure Cook. Select High Pressure; set timer for 9 minutes.
4 When time is up, use quick release. Unlock lid.
5 Stir with fork to separate pasta. Serve with grated Parmesan cheese and garnish, as desired.

Spaghetti & Meatballs

QUICK TIP

If you want to make
your own meatballs,
use a mix of meats
(pork, beef, veal).
And yes: You can
make them in the
Instant Pot!

**Korean Barbecue
Beef Over Noodles**

Korean Barbecue Beef Over Noodles

Look for Asian noodles (such as lo mein, soba, udon or pad thai) in your supermarket for an authentic dish. Can't find any? Just sub in spaghetti or rice instead.

START TO FINISH 25 minutes
(10 minutes active)

SERVINGS 6

INGREDIENTS

- ½ cup beef stock
- ⅓ cup soy sauce
- ⅓ cup brown sugar
- 1 teaspoon minced garlic
- 1 tablespoon sesame oil
- 1 tablespoon rice wine vinegar
- 1 tablespoon grated ginger
- 1 teaspoon Sriracha sauce
- 2 pounds beef stew meat, cut in 1-inch cubes
- 3 tablespoons cornstarch
- 3 tablespoons water
   Hot cooked noodles
   Garnish: sliced scallions

1 In a large bowl, combine beef stock, soy sauce, brown sugar, garlic, sesame oil, rice wine vinegar, ginger and Sriracha sauce.
2 Stir in beef and place in Instant Pot.
3 Lock lid; set pressure release valve to Sealing. Select Pressure Cook. Select High Pressure; set timer for 15 minutes.
4 When time is up, use quick release. Unlock lid.
5 In a small bowl, whisk together cornstarch and water.
6 Select Sauté; whisk in cornstarch mixture, stirring frequently, until sauce is thickened.
7 Serve over hot noodles and garnish, as desired.

Quick Jambalaya

This Louisiana favorite cooks up amazingly quickly in an Instant Pot.

START TO FINISH 30 minutes
(10 minutes active)

SERVINGS 6

INGREDIENTS

- 1 tablespoon vegetable oil
- 1 onion, chopped
- 1 red bell pepper, chopped
- 2   cups chicken broth
- 1 teaspoon minced garlic
- 1 (16-ounce) package andouille sausage, sliced
- 1 tablespoon Creole seasoning
- 1 (15-ounce) can diced tomatoes
- 1½ cups white rice, rinsed
- 1 tablespoon Worcestershire sauce
- 1 teaspoon hot sauce
   Garnishes: sliced scallions, chopped parsley

1 On an Instant Pot, select Sauté; heat oil. Add onion and bell pepper and cook for 3 minutes.
2 Stir in chicken broth, scraping up any of the brown bits in the bottom of the pot.
3 Stir in garlic, sausage, Creole seasoning, tomatoes and rice.
4 Lock lid; set pressure release valve to Sealing. Select Pressure Cook. Select High Pressure; set timer for 5 minutes.
5 When time is up, use natural release for 10 minutes, then quick-release remaining pressure. Unlock lid.
6 Stir in Worcestershire and hot sauce. Garnish, as desired.

Pork Tenderloin With Thyme Gravy

This cut of meat can turn dry and tough if cooked incorrectly—but that won't happen in the Instant Pot! Thyme is a perfect complement here.

START TO FINISH 30 minutes
(15 minutes active)

SERVINGS 4

INGREDIENTS

- 1 teaspoon salt
- 1 teaspoon ground black pepper
- ½ teaspoon Italian seasoning
- 1 (2-pound) pork tenderloin, cut in half
- 1 tablespoon olive oil
- 2 cups chicken stock
- 2 tablespoons lemon juice
- 1 tablespoon soy sauce
- 3 tablespoons cornstarch
- 3 tablespoons water
- 2 teaspoons thyme leaves
   Garnish: thyme sprigs

1 In a small bowl, combine salt, pepper and Italian seasoning.
2 Rub on all sides of pork.
3 On an Instant Pot, select Sauté; heat oil. Brown sides of pork, about 3 minutes per side.
4 Remove pork and set aside.
5 Pour in chicken stock, lemon juice and soy sauce, stirring to combine.
6 Place steam rack in Instant Pot. Place pork on rack.
7 Lock lid; set pressure release valve to Sealing. Select Pressure Cook. Select High Pressure; set timer for 6 minutes.
8 When time is up, use natural release for 10 minutes, then quick-release remaining pressure. Unlock lid.
9 Remove pork to cutting board to rest 5 minutes.
10 Press Sauté again. Combine cornstarch and water in small bowl.
11 Whisk into Instant Pot and stir until thickened. Stir in thyme leaves.
12 Serve gravy with pork.

Rosemary Pork Loin Chops

with 1 tablespoon cold water. Add to boiling liquid in pot and whisk until mixture thickens into gravy. Add butter and remaining rosemary to gravy. Garnish chops with rosemary sprigs and serve gravy on the side.

Beef Stroganoff With Egg Noodles

Use your favorite mushrooms in this hearty, creamy dish.

START TO FINISH 30 minutes
(15 minutes active)

SERVINGS 4-6

INGREDIENTS

- $1/4$ cup butter
- 2 teaspoons minced garlic
- 2 cups sliced mushrooms
- $1/4$ cup flour
- 1 teaspoon salt
- $1/2$ teaspoon ground black pepper
- $3 1/4$ cups beef broth, divided
- $1/4$ cup Worcestershire sauce
- 2 pounds beef stew meat
- 1 (12-ounce) package egg noodles
- $1/2$ cup sour cream
- 2 tablespoons cornstarch
  Garnish: chopped parsley

1 On an Instant Pot, select Sauté; melt butter. Add garlic and mushrooms. Sprinkle with flour, salt and pepper.

2 Add 3 cups broth, Worcestershire sauce and beef.

3 Lock lid; set pressure release valve to Sealing. Select Pressure Cook. Select High Pressure; set timer for 15 minutes.

4 When time is up, use quick release. Unlock lid. Add noodles to pot.

5 Lock lid again; set pressure release valve to Sealing. Select Pressure Cook. Select High Pressure; set timer for 3 minutes. Use quick release again.

6 Unlock pot; stir in sour cream. Select Soup setting.

7 Combine cornstarch and remaining $1/4$ cup broth in a small bowl. Stir into stroganoff mixture until thickened. Sprinkle with chopped parsley and serve.

MORE TIME BUT WORTH IT

Rosemary Pork Loin Chops

Rosemary and pork are a classic combo, and this pan gravy is so rich.

START TO FINISH 40 minutes
(10 minutes active)

SERVINGS 2

INGREDIENTS

- 2 (1-pound) pork loin chops
- $1 1/2$ teaspoons kosher salt, divided
- 1 teaspoon black pepper, divided
- 2 tablespoons chopped fresh rosemary, divided
- 2 tablespoons olive oil
- 1 cup sliced yellow onion
- $1/2$ cup chicken stock
- 1 tablespoon cornstarch
- 3 tablespoons butter
  Garnish: rosemary sprigs

1 Season chops on all sides with $3/4$ teaspoon salt, $1/2$ teaspoon pepper and 1 tablespoon chopped fresh rosemary.

2 On an Instant Pot, select Sauté; heat oil. Add chops, searing on all sides until browned, about 3 minutes per side.

3 Remove chops from pot; pour off fat. Add onion, remaining salt, remaining pepper and $1/2$ teaspoon rosemary; cook while stirring for 1 minute or until onions have softened. Add chicken stock and stir, scraping any browned bits from the bottom of the pot.

4 Add chops back to pot. Lock lid; set pressure release valve to Sealing. Select Pressure Cook. Select High Pressure; set timer for 17 minutes.

5 When time is up, use quick release. Unlock lid.

6 Place chops on cutting board; let stand 10 minutes. Meanwhile, select Sauté; bring liquid in pot to a boil.

7 In a small bowl, mix cornstarch

Beef Tacos

Queso fresco is a mild, crumbly cheese that's similar to feta (but less salty); it's easy to find in most grocery stores.

START TO FINISH 30 minutes (10 minutes active)

SERVINGS 4

INGREDIENTS

- 2 tablespoons canola oil
- 1½ pounds chuck steak, cut into 2-inch pieces
- 1 teaspoon kosher salt
- 1½ cups beef stock
- 1 (15-ounce) can diced tomatoes with chiles
- 2 tablespoons chopped chipotle in adobo
- 8 (6-inch) flour tortillas
- 1 avocado, sliced
- ½ cup pico de gallo
- ½ cup crumbled queso fresco cheese
- ½ cup cilantro leaves
  Garnish: lime wedges

1 In an Instant Pot, add oil; select Sauté. Season beef with salt; add to pot. Cook, turning once, until browned, about 3 minutes. Add stock, tomatoes and chipotle. Select Cancel.

2 Lock lid; set pressure release valve to Sealing. Select High Pressure on manual; set timer for 15 minutes.

3 When time is up, use quick release. Unlock lid. Remove beef; place on cutting board and use 2 forks to shred.

4 On each tortilla, spread ¼ cup beef; top with avocado, pico de gallo, cheese and cilantro. Serve with lime wedges on the side.

POULTRY

YOU'LL BE DELIGHTED TO
DISCOVER JUST HOW MOIST CHICKEN
CAN BE WHEN IT'S COOKED
IN AN INSTANT POT!

Thai Chicken
Wraps, page 54

Thai Chicken Wraps

Using lettuce instead of a flour wrap gives this meal a fresh and crunchy edge; precooked chicken saves even more time.

START TO FINISH 30 minutes
(15 minutes active)
SERVINGS 4–6

INGREDIENTS

$1^{1}/_{2}$ cups quinoa, rinsed and drained
2 cups water
$^{1}/_{8}$ teaspoon salt
$^{1}/_{4}$ cup fresh lime juice
$^{1}/_{4}$ cup peanut oil
2 teaspoons soy sauce
1 teaspoon fish sauce
1 teaspoon sugar
$^{1}/_{8}$ to $^{1}/_{4}$ teaspoon crushed red pepper
1 small clove garlic, minced
2 tablespoons chopped scallions (green part only)
1 stalk lemongrass (white part only), chopped
1 medium seedless cucumber, thinly sliced on the bias
2 medium carrots, thinly sliced on the bias
2 cups leftover shredded chicken or turkey
1 head bibb lettuce, leaves separated
$^{1}/_{2}$ cup fresh loosely packed basil leaves
$^{1}/_{3}$ cup loosely packed fresh mint leaves
$^{1}/_{2}$ cup peanuts, coarsely chopped
Garnish: lime wedges

1 In an Instant Pot, stir quinoa, water and salt. Lock lid; set pressure release valve to Sealing. Select Pressure Cook. Select High Pressure; set timer for 2 minutes.
2 When time is up, use quick release. Unlock lid.
3 Meanwhile, make dressing: In a small bowl, whisk lime juice, peanut oil, soy sauce, fish sauce, sugar, red pepper, garlic, scallions and lemongrass until sugar dissolves.
4 Spread cooked quinoa in a shallow pan and let cool for 5 minutes. In a large bowl, combine quinoa, cucumber, carrots and chicken. Drizzle with dressing; toss to coat.
5 Divide among lettuce leaves. Top with basil, mint leaves and peanuts. Serve with lime wedges.

Chicken Alfredo

Rich, cheesy, garlicky—what's not to love about this classic dish?

START TO FINISH 25 minutes
(15 minutes active)
SERVINGS 4

INGREDIENTS

$^{1}/_{4}$ cup butter, divided
4 boneless, skinless chicken breasts, cubed
$^{1}/_{2}$ teaspoon salt
$^{1}/_{2}$ teaspoon ground black pepper
1 teaspoon minced garlic
2 cups chicken broth
8 ounces fettuccine, broken in half
1 cup heavy cream
$^{2}/_{3}$ cup grated Parmesan cheese
Garnishes: chopped parsley, grated Parmesan

1 On an Instant Pot, select Sauté; melt butter. Add chicken; sprinkle with salt and pepper. Cook 3 minutes, stirring; add garlic and cook 1 minute.
2 Remove mixture from pot; set aside. Stir in broth; scrape bottom of pot with a wooden spoon to deglaze.
3 Add pasta to pot. Add water to cover. Add chicken mixture on top.
4 Lock lid; set pressure release valve to Sealing. Select Pressure Cook. Select High Pressure; set timer for 5 minutes.
5 When time is up, use natural release for 5 minutes, then quick-release remaining pressure. Unlock lid.
6 Remove chicken from pot; using tongs or forks, separate pasta strands.
7 Select Sauté. Stir in cream and Parmesan. Cook, stirring, for 2 minutes or until thickened. Return chicken to the pot to reheat.
8 Serve, garnished as desired.

Cheesy Chicken & Broccoli With Rice

Comfort food at its best, this casserolelike dish comes together quickly, with an easy cleanup!

START TO FINISH 30 minutes
(10 minutes active)

SERVINGS 4–6

INGREDIENTS

- 1 cup chicken broth
- 1 (10.5-ounce) can condensed cream of chicken soup
- 8 ounces small cremini mushrooms, washed, stem ends trimmed, and cut in half
- 2 cups cooked chopped chicken or turkey
- 2 cups coarsely chopped fresh broccoli florets
- 2 cups shredded cheddar cheese (8 ounces)
- 2 (8.8-ounce) packages cooked rice, heated according to package directions
- 3 tablespoons sliced almonds, toasted
- 2 scallions, sliced

1 In an Instant Pot, stir broth, soup, mushrooms, chicken and broccoli.
2 Lock lid; set pressure release valve to Sealing. Select Pressure Cook. Select High Pressure; set timer for 2 minutes.
3 When time is up, use quick release. Unlock lid.
4 Stir cheese into pot until melted.
5 Serve over rice. Sprinkle with toasted almonds and scallions.

Chicken Curry

Chicken Curry

Good-quality curry powder is key to the taste of this dish. Coconut milk keeps the flavors well balanced.

START TO FINISH 25 minutes
(15 minutes active)

SERVINGS 4

INGREDIENTS

- 3 tablespoons olive oil
- 1 pound chicken breast, cubed
- 1 onion, chopped
- 1 carrot, sliced
- 1 bell pepper, sliced
- 6 new potatoes, quartered
- ¼ cup curry powder
- 1 (13.6-ounce) can coconut milk
- 1 tablespoon minced ginger
- 1 teaspoon salt
- ½ teaspoon ground black pepper
- 2 teaspoons cornstarch
- 1 tablespoon water
   Hot cooked jasmine rice
   Garnish: cilantro leaves

1 On an Instant Pot, select Sauté; heat oil. Add chicken and cook 5 minutes or until browned. Turn pot off.
2 Add onion and next 8 ingredients.
3 Lock lid; set pressure release valve to Sealing. Select Pressure Cook. Select High Pressure; set timer for 5 minutes.
4 When time is up, use natural release for 10 minutes, then quick-release remaining pressure. Unlock lid.
5 Select Sauté; whisk together cornstarch and water. Stir into Instant Pot and cook 1 minute.
6 Serve over rice and garnish with cilantro leaves.

QUICK TIP

Which rice to use? Jasmine rice has a shorter grain and cooks up softer and stickier; basmati rice has a longer, thinner grain and cooks up fluffier and firmer.

Quick Chicken & Noodles

Quick Chicken & Noodles

The name says it all—this comes together without muss or fuss.

START TO FINISH 30 minutes
(5 minutes active)

SERVINGS 6

INGREDIENTS

- 1 (16-ounce) package egg noodles
- 3 cups water
- ½ teaspoon salt
- ¼ teaspoon ground black pepper
- 3 cups chopped cooked chicken
- 2 carrots, peeled and sliced
- 3 (10.5-ounce) cans cream of mushroom soup or cream of chicken soup
- 1 tablespoon Dijon mustard
- 1 teaspoon dried parsley

1 In an Instant Pot, add noodles. Stir in remaining ingredients.
2 Lock lid; set pressure release valve to Sealing. Select Pressure Cook. Select High Pressure; set timer for 4 minutes.
3 When time is up, use quick release. Unlock lid. Stir before serving.

Foolproof Chicken Breasts

Any leftovers? Chop them to make chicken salad for lunch the next day.

START TO FINISH 30 minutes
(5 minutes active)

SERVINGS 4

INGREDIENTS

- 2 teaspoons Italian seasoning
- 1 teaspoon salt
- ½ teaspoon ground black pepper
- ½ teaspoon garlic powder
- 2 tablespoons olive oil, divided
- 4 boneless, skinless chicken breasts
- 1 cup chicken broth

1 In a small bowl, combine Italian seasoning, salt, pepper and garlic powder. Stir in 1 tablespoon of olive oil. Rub paste over the chicken breasts.
2 On an Instant Pot, select Sauté; heat remaining oil. Add chicken and cook for 2 minutes per side. Remove and set aside.
3 Pour chicken broth into pot; use a wooden spoon to scrape up any browned bits on the bottom of pot.
4 Place steam rack in pot; place chicken on rack in a single layer.
5 Lock lid; set pressure release valve to Sealing. Select Pressure Cook. Select High Pressure; set timer for 5 minutes.
6 When time is up, use natural release for 8 minutes, then quick-release remaining pressure. Unlock lid.
7 Remove chicken from pot; let rest for 5 minutes before serving.

White Chicken Chili

White Chicken Chili

Chicken makes a nice switch from beef in this delicious, filling dish. If you like it spicy, add a sliced jalapeño or a small can of roasted green chiles.

START TO FINISH 30 minutes
(10 minutes active)

SERVINGS 6

INGREDIENTS

- 1 boneless, skinless chicken breast, cubed
- 2 cups chicken broth
- 1 (14.5-ounce) can white navy beans, drained and rinsed
- 1 (10-ounce) bag frozen roasted corn
- 1 onion, chopped
- 1 green bell pepper, chopped
- 1 tablespoon chili powder
- 1 teaspoon salt
- 4 ounces cream cheese, cubed
  Garnishes: sour cream, grated cheese, avocado, cilantro leaves, sliced jalapeño

1 Place cubed chicken and next 7 ingredients in Instant Pot and stir.
2 Lock lid; set pressure release valve to Sealing. Select Pressure Cook. Select High Pressure; set timer for 10 minutes.
3 When time is up, use natural release for 10 minutes, then quick-release remaining pressure. Unlock lid.
4 Stir in cream cheese until smooth.
5 Garnish as desired to serve.

Orange Sesame Chicken

This Chinese restaurant favorite is surprisingly easy to duplicate at home with an Instant Pot.

START TO FINISH 30 minutes
(15 minutes active)

SERVINGS 6

INGREDIENTS

- 1 tablespoon vegetable oil
- 1 tablespoon sesame oil
- 4 boneless, skinless chicken breasts, cubed
- 1 cup + 3 tablespoons fresh orange juice, divided
- 1 tablespoon grated ginger
- 1 tablespoon minced garlic
- 1 tablespoon white wine
- $^1/_2$ cup tomato sauce
- $^1/_3$ cup brown sugar
- $^1/_3$ cup soy sauce
- 1 tablespoon Sriracha sauce
- 3 tablespoons cornstarch
  Hot cooked white rice
  Garnishes: sliced scallions, orange zest, sesame seeds

1 On an Instant Pot, select Sauté; heat oils. Add chicken; cook and stir for about 5 minutes. Add 1 cup orange juice, ginger, garlic, wine, tomato sauce, sugar, soy sauce and Sriracha; mix well.
2 Lock lid; set pressure release valve to Sealing. Select Pressure Cook. Select High Pressure; set timer for 5 minutes.
3 When time is up, use natural release for 10 minutes, then quick-release remaining pressure. Unlock lid.
4 In a small bowl, whisk together cornstarch and remaining orange juice.
5 Select Sauté; stir in cornstarch mixture and simmer for 4 minutes or until thickened.
6 Place rice on serving plates; top with chicken and garnish, as desired.

Chicken Tikka Masala

Naan, a soft, leavened flatbread, is perfect for serving on the side of this creamy, flavorful dish.

START TO FINISH 30 minutes
(15 minutes active)

SERVINGS 4

INGREDIENTS

- 1 tablespoon butter
- 1 onion, chopped
- 1 tablespoon minced ginger
- 1 tablespoon minced garlic
- 2 tablespoons garam masala
- 1 teaspoon cumin
- 1 teaspoon salt
- ½ teaspoon red pepper flakes
- 2 pounds chicken breasts, cubed
- 1 (15-ounce) can tomato sauce
- ½ cup heavy cream, divided
- 2 tablespoons chopped cilantro
  - Hot basmati rice
  - Warm naan

1 On an Instant Pot, select Sauté; heat butter. Add onion, ginger and garlic, cook 3 minutes. Stir in garam masala, cumin, salt and red pepper flakes.

2 Add chicken, tomato sauce and ¼ cup cream.

3 Lock lid; set pressure release valve to Sealing. Select Pressure Cook. Select High Pressure; set timer for 8 minutes.

4 When time is up, use natural release for 10 minutes, then quick-release remaining pressure. Unlock lid.

5 Remove chicken from pot. Select Sauté; add remaining cream to pot and cook until thickened, about 8 minutes. Stir in chicken and cilantro.

6 Serve over rice, with naan on the side.

Butter Chicken

A touch of cream will make this Indian-inspired dish a hit!

START TO FINISH 20 minutes
(5 minutes active)

SERVINGS 6

INGREDIENTS

- 1 (28-ounce) can crushed tomatoes
- ⅔ cup dry white wine
- ¼ cup butter
- 1 cup chopped onion
- 2 tablespoons curry powder
- 1 tablespoon minced ginger
- ½ teaspoon kosher salt
- ¼ teaspoon ground black pepper
- 4 boneless, skinless chicken thighs, chopped
- ⅓ cup heavy cream
- 2 cups cooked basmati rice
  Garnishes: cilantro leaves, sliced chives

1 On an Instant Pot, select Sauté; add tomatoes, wine, butter, onion, curry powder, ginger, salt and pepper to pot. Cook, stirring occasionally, about 2 minutes.

2 Turn off Sauté function; add chicken thighs and toss well in sauce to coat. Lock lid; set pressure release valve to Sealing. Select Pressure Cook. Select High Pressure; set timer for 15 minutes.

3 When time is up, use quick release. Unlock lid. Transfer chicken to a bowl (leave sauce in pot).

4 Select Sauté; set timer for 5 minutes. Bring sauce to a simmer. Stir in cream; cook until sauce is slightly thickened, about 2 minutes. Turn off Sauté function; stir in chicken. Serve over rice and garnish, as desired.

Honey Sesame Chicken

It doesn't take much sesame oil to impart amazing flavor to this Asian-inspired chicken.

START TO FINISH 35 minutes
(5 minutes active)

SERVINGS 6

INGREDIENTS

- 1 tablespoon olive oil
- 2 pounds boneless skinless chicken thighs
- 1/2 cup diced onion
- 2 cloves minced garlic
- 1/2 cup soy sauce
- 1/4 cup tomato paste
- 1/4 teaspoon red pepper flakes
- 1/3 cup honey
- 1 tablespoon sesame oil
- 2 tablespoons cornstarch
  Hot cooked rice
  Garnishes: sliced scallions, white and black sesame seeds

Honey Sesame Chicken

1 On an Instant Pot, select Sauté; heat olive oil. Add chicken; brown on both sides, 4 minutes per side. Place chicken in a shallow dish; cover with foil.
2 Add onion to pot; cook until soft, 4 minutes. Add garlic; cook for 1 minute more. Add soy sauce, tomato paste and red pepper flakes; use a wooden spoon to scrape browned bits from bottom of pot. Select Cancel.
3 Return chicken to pot. Lock lid; set pressure release valve to Sealing. Select Pressure Cook. Select High Pressure; set timer for 5 minutes.
4 When time is up, use natural release for 5 minutes, then quick-release remaining pressure. Unlock lid.
5 Cut chicken into bite-size pieces.
6 Add honey and sesame oil to pot; stir to combine.
7 In a small bowl mix together 1/4 cup of hot liquid from pot and cornstarch. Pour into pot; stir until thickened. Add chicken back to pot; stir to coat.
8 Serve over rice and garnish, as desired.

Ranch Chicken Sandwiches

Between the bacon, the ranch dressing and not one but two cheeses in these shredded chicken sandwiches, you may have found your family's new favorite meal. Be sure to have plenty of napkins on hand, too!

START TO FINISH 25 minutes
(5 minutes active)

SERVINGS 6

INGREDIENTS

- 1/2 pound bacon, chopped
- 1 cup chicken broth
- 1 (1-ounce) packet ranch seasoning
- 1 pound boneless and skinless chicken breasts
- 1 (8-ounce) package cream cheese, cut into chunks
- 1 tablespoon cornstarch
- 1/2 cup shredded cheddar cheese
- 1/4 cup sliced scallions
- 6 hamburger buns
  Pickle slices (optional)

1 On an Instant Pot, select Sauté. Add bacon to pot; cook 5 minutes. Remove bacon and drain between paper towels. Set aside 1/4 cup to top sandwiches.
2 Add broth to pot; deglaze, using a wooden spoon to scrape up any browned bits. Whisk ranch seasoning into broth. Add chicken to pot; top with cream cheese.
3 Lock lid; set pressure release valve to Sealing. Select Pressure Cook. Select High Pressure; set timer for 15 minutes.
4 When time is up, use natural release for 10 minutes, then quick-release remaining pressure. Unlock lid.
5 Place chicken on cutting board and use 2 forks to shred chicken.
6 Whisk cornstarch into sauce in pot. Add chicken and non-reserved bacon to pot; mix until evenly coated.
7 Divide mixture evenly between buns; top evenly with cheddar, scallions, reserved bacon and pickle slices, as desired.

Chicken Piccata

oil. Add chicken; brown for 3 minutes on each side. Remove from pot.

4 Add broth to pot; scrape up any browned bits from pot. Add butter, chicken, capers and lemon juice.

5 Lock lid; set pressure release valve to Sealing. Select Pressure Cook. Select High Pressure; set timer for 4 minutes.

6 When time is up, use natural release for 10 minutes, then quick-release remaining pressure.

7 In a small bowl, whisk together cornstarch and water; add to sauce in pot. Select Sauté; cook for 2 minutes until thickened.

8 Place chicken on serving plate; spoon sauce over the top. Garnish, as desired.

Spicy Chicken Tacos

Wrap the tortillas in foil and keep warm in a low oven while this cooks.

START TO FINISH 25 minutes
(10 minutes active)
SERVINGS 4

INGREDIENTS

- 1 cup chicken broth
- 2 tablespoons taco seasoning
- 1 teaspoon cayenne pepper
- 2 bone-in, skinless chicken breasts
- 8 (6-inch) flour tortillas, warmed
- 1 cup shredded iceberg lettuce
- 1 cup pico de gallo
- ½ cup sour cream
- ½ cup crumbled queso fresco cheese
    Garnish: cilantro sprigs

1 In an Instant Pot, whisk broth, taco seasoning and cayenne. Add chicken. Lock lid; set pressure release valve to Sealing. Select Pressure Cook. Select High Pressure; set timer for 12 minutes.

2 When time is up, use quick release. Unlock lid. Remove chicken from pot. Using 2 forks, remove chicken from bones and shred. Add back to pot.

3 Place 2 tortillas on each serving plate. Divide chicken evenly among tortillas; top with remaining ingredients. Garnish with cilantro.

MORE TIME BUT WORTH IT

Chicken Piccata

Serve this with pasta or risotto to soak up the tangy lemon-caper butter.

START TO FINISH 35 minutes
(15 minutes active)
SERVINGS 4

INGREDIENTS

- 1½ pounds boneless chicken breast
- 1 teaspoon salt
- ½ teaspoon ground black pepper
- ¼ cup all-purpose flour
- ¼ cup panko breadcrumbs
- ¼ cup finely grated Parmesan cheese
- 1 teaspoon dried oregano
- 1 teaspoon dried basil
- 3 tablespoons olive oil
- 1¼ cups chicken broth
- 2 tablespoons butter
- ¼ cup capers
- ¼ cup fresh lemon juice
- 2 tablespoons cornstarch
- ¼ cup cold water
    Garnish: chopped parsley

1 Season chicken on both sides with salt and pepper.

2 In a bowl, mix flour, breadcrumbs, Parmesan, oregano and basil. Dredge each chicken piece in flour mixture.

3 On an Instant Pot, select Sauté; heat

Spicy
Chicken
Tacos

QUICK TIP

If you frequently
serve tacos, consider
getting a taco rack
that holds the shells
upright after they've
been filled.

63

MORE TIME BUT WORTH IT

Teriyaki Chicken Thighs

Use your favorite teriyaki marinade. Cooking with pressure will make the thighs incredibly tender and moist.

START TO FINISH 35 minutes
(10 minutes active)

SERVINGS 4

INGREDIENTS

- 2 tablespoons olive oil
- 4 boneless, skinless chicken thighs
- 1 cup sesame teriyaki marinade
- 1½ tablespoons cornstarch
- 1 tablespoon water
  Hot cooked rice
  Garnish: sliced scallions

1 On an Instant Pot, select Sauté; heat oil to warm. Add chicken; cook about 4 minutes on each side or until browned. Remove chicken; set aside.

2 Add ¼ cup water to pot; use a wooden spoon to scrape browned bits from the bottom of pot. Return chicken to pot; pour in 1½ cups water and teriyaki marinade.

3 Lock lid; set pressure release valve to Sealing. Select Pressure Cook. Select High Pressure; set timer for 16 minutes.

4 When time is up, use natural release. Remove chicken; set aside.

5 Select Sauté. In a small bowl, whisk cornstarch and water. Pour cornstarch mixture into pot; stir until slightly thickened.

6 Place rice on serving platter; top with chicken and pour sauce from pot over top. Garnish, as desired.

Peanut Chicken
Cabbage Cups

Peanut Chicken
Cabbage Cups

These Thai-inspired cups are not
too spicy, but they're full of flavor.

START TO FINISH 25 minutes
(10 minutes active)

SERVINGS 4

INGREDIENTS

3 tablespoons soy sauce
1 tablespoon honey
1 teaspoon grated ginger
1 clove garlic, sliced
2 teaspoons chili-garlic sauce
2 tablespoons water
1 pound ground chicken
1 small red onion, sliced
1 small head cabbage, leaves
   separated
1 cup matchstick carrots
1/2 cup thinly sliced watermelon
   radish
1/4 cup chopped roasted peanuts
   Lime wedges

1 In an Instant Pot, stir together
soy sauce, honey, ginger, garlic,
chili-garlic sauce and water. Stir in
chicken and onion.
2 Lock lid; set pressure release valve
to Sealing. Select Pressure Cook. Select
High Pressure; set timer for 9 minutes.

3 When time is up, use natural
release. stir mixture.
4 Select Sauté; cook until chicken is
done, about 5 minutes.
5 Spoon mixture into cabbage
leaves; top with carrots, radishes and
peanuts. Serve with lime wedges.

MORE TIME BUT WORTH IT

Creamy Chicken
& Dumplings

Colorful and comforting, chicken
and dumplings is always a favorite
dish. Frozen dumplings can be found
in many major supermarkets; they're
a huge time-saver!

START TO FINISH 45 minutes
(15 minutes active)

SERVINGS 6

INGREDIENTS

1 tablespoon olive oil
1 onion, chopped
1 teaspoon minced garlic
1 russet potato, cubed
3 carrots, sliced in 1-inch pieces
2 celery ribs
1 teaspoon salt
1 teaspoon ground black pepper
1/2 cup flour

2 bay leaves
2 thyme sprigs
6 boneless, skinless chicken
   breasts
4 cups chicken stock
1 (24-ounce) package frozen
   dumplings
1 cup frozen green peas, thawed
2/3 cup heavy cream
   Garnish: chopped parsley

1 On an Instant Pot, select Sauté;
heat oil. Add onion and garlic and
cook 2 minutes. Add potato, carrots,
celery, salt and pepper.
2 Whisk in flour and cook 1 minute.
3 Stir in bay leaves and thyme sprigs.
4 Add chicken, stock and dumplings.
5 Lock lid; set pressure release valve
to Sealing. Select Soup; set timer
for 7 minutes.
6 When time is up, use natural
release for 10 minutes, then
quick-release remaining pressure.
Unlock lid.
7 Remove chicken and place on
cutting board; shred with 2 forks.
8 Return chicken to pot; stir in peas
and cream.
9 Select Sauté and cook for 2 minutes
or until everything is cooked through.
10 Garnish with parsley.

SEAFOOD

THESE SAVORY SHELLFISH AND FISH RECIPES
WILL HAVE YOU REACHING FOR YOUR
INSTANT POT OVER AND OVER!

Simple Steamed
Salmon Fillets,
page 72

Shrimp Scampi

Seafood Paella

This showstopping Spanish classic is a meal in itself, making it ideal for summer dinner parties or whenever you need a crowd-pleasing dish.

START TO FINISH 30 minutes
(20 minutes active)

SERVINGS 4

INGREDIENTS

- 4 tablespoons butter
- 1 cup chopped onion
- 6 cloves garlic, chopped
- 1 teaspoon hot paprika
- 1 teaspoon ground turmeric
- ½ teaspoon kosher salt
- ¼ teaspoon ground black pepper
- ¼ teaspoon crushed red pepper flakes
- 1 pinch saffron threads
- 1 cup uncooked arborio rice
- 1 red bell pepper, sliced
- 1 cup chicken stock
- ½ cup white wine
- 1 pound large shrimp, peeled and deveined
- 1 pound small sea scallops
- 1 cup frozen green peas
   Garnishes: chopped cilantro, chopped parsley

1 On an Instant Pot, select Sauté. Add butter and onion; cook until onion is soft, 4 minutes. Add garlic; cook 1 more minute. Add paprika, turmeric, salt, black pepper, red pepper flakes and saffron; cook about 1 more minute. Add rice and bell pepper; stir well.

2 Add stock and wine; use a wooden spoon to scrape up any browned bits from bottom of pot. Select Cancel.

3 Lock lid; set pressure release valve to Sealing. Select Pressure Cook. Select High Pressure; set timer for 6 minutes.

4 When time is up, use quick release. Unlock lid.

5 Add shrimp, scallops and peas. Select Sauté; cook, stirring, until shrimp and scallops are cooked through and most of the liquid has been absorbed, about 3 minutes.

6 Place on serving platter; garnish, as desired.

Shrimp Scampi

Angel hair cooks very quickly, so don't prepare it too early.

START TO FINISH 15 minutes
(5 minutes active)

SERVINGS 4

INGREDIENTS

- ¾ cup dry white wine
- 3 tablespoons butter
- 2 tablespoons olive oil
- 1 tablespoon minced garlic
- ½ teaspoon dried oregano
- ½ teaspoon red pepper flakes
- 2 pounds medium shrimp, peeled and deveined with tails on
- 8 ounces angel hair pasta
   Garnish: oregano sprigs

1 In an Instant Pot, stir together wine, butter, oil, garlic, oregano and red pepper flakes. Stir in shrimp.

2 Lock lid; set pressure release valve to Sealing. Select Pressure Cook. Select High Pressure; set timer for 6 minutes.

3 Meanwhile, cook pasta according to package directions.

4 When time is up, use quick release. Unlock lid.

5 In a bowl, add pasta, shrimp and sauce; gently toss. Garnish with oregano.

Scallops Alfredo

Scallops make this creamy classic taste even more special.

START TO FINISH 15 minutes
(10 minutes active)

SERVINGS 4

INGREDIENTS

 1   (16-ounce) jar Alfredo sauce, divided
2¹/₂   cups chicken broth
 ¹/₂   teaspoon dried oregano
 ¹/₂   teaspoon garlic powder
 ¹/₂   teaspoon red pepper flakes
 1   (12-ounce) bag dried fettuccine pasta
 1   pound frozen large scallops
 1   cup frozen peas
     Garnishes: parsley leaves, cracked black pepper

1 In an Instant Pot, add 1¹/₂ cups of sauce. Stir in broth, oregano, garlic powder and pepper flakes until smooth. Stir in fettuccine. Arrange frozen scallops on top.

2 Lock lid; set pressure release valve to Sealing. Select Pressure Cook. Select High Pressure; set timer for 4 minutes.

3 When time is up, use natural release for 1 minute, then quick-release remaining pressure. Unlock lid.

4 Stir in remaining sauce and peas. Serve hot and garnish, as desired.

**Lowcountry
Seafood Feast**

Lowcountry Seafood Feast

This Southern favorite offers up a little something for everyone.

START TO FINISH 1 hour, 15 minutes
(50 minutes active)

SERVINGS 6

INGREDIENTS

- 1 pound small red potatoes, halved
- 1 pound smoked sausage, cut into 1-inch pieces
- 4 ears corn, shucked; quartered
- 4 garlic cloves, chopped, divided
- 2 tablespoons Cajun seasoning, divided
- 4 bay leaves
- 1 (12-ounce) can of beer
- 1 pound medium shrimp
- 3 tablespoons butter
- 2 tablespoons chopped parsley
- 2 lemons, divided
  Garnish: chopped parsley

1 In Instant Pot, combine potatoes, sausage, corn, 3 chopped garlic cloves, 1½ tablespoons Cajun seasoning, bay leaves and beer.
2 Lock lid; set pressure release valve to Sealing. Select Pressure Cook. Select High Pressure; set timer for 45 minutes.
3 When time is up, use quick release. Unlock lid; use a slotted spoon to place pot contents on serving platter.
4 Select Sauté; bring pot liquid to a boil. Add shrimp; cook until just cooked through, about 4 minutes. Select Cancel.
5 Lock lid; set pressure release valve to Sealing. Select Pressure Cook. Select High Pressure; set timer for 1 minute.
6 When time is up, use quick release. Unlock lid; use slotted spoon to put shrimp on serving platter.
7 Select Sauté; cook to reduce liquid slightly, about 2 minutes.
8 Stir butter, parsley, remaining garlic, remaining Cajun seasoning and juice of 1 lemon into pot.
9 Pour sauce onto serving platter. Cut remaining lemon into 6 wedges and serve, garnished with parsley.

Mango Fish Tacos

Warm the tortillas before serving by wrapping a stack in foil and placing in a 350 F oven for 10 to 15 minutes.

START TO FINISH 40 minutes
(30 minutes active)

SERVINGS 4

INGREDIENTS

- 1 teaspoon kosher salt
- 1 teaspoon garlic powder
- 1 teaspoon smoked paprika
- ½ teaspoon ground black pepper
- 1 pound flounder fillets, cut into chunks
- 1 cup cubed fresh mango
- 2 teaspoons hot sauce
- ⅓ cup barbecue sauce
- 2 tablespoons olive oil
- 1 tablespoon lemon juice
- 1 tablespoon mayonnaise
- ½ teaspoon salt
- ½ cup shredded purple cabbage
  Warm corn tortillas
  Garnishes: cubed mango, cilantro sprigs, sliced jalapeño

1 In a small bowl, mix salt, garlic powder, paprika and pepper. In a medium bowl, place fish; sprinkle seasoning mixture over pieces and let sit for 15 minutes.
2 In a food processor, combine mango, hot sauce and barbecue sauce until smooth. Set aside.
3 On an Instant Pot, select Sauté; heat oil. Add fish in a single layer; cook 2 minutes until brown, then flip and cook 2 minutes on other side. Stir in mango mixture. Select Cancel.
4 Lock lid; set pressure release valve to Sealing. Select Pressure Cook. Select High Pressure; set timer for 5 minutes.
5 Meanwhile, in a medium bowl, stir together lemon juice, mayonnaise and salt; add cabbage and toss to make slaw.
6 When time is up, use natural release for 3 minutes, then quick-release remaining pressure. Unlock lid.
7 Place warm tortillas on serving plates; top with fish and slaw. Garnish, as desired.

Simple Steamed Salmon Fillets

Wine, lemon and dill season these fillets to perfection.

START TO FINISH 15 minutes
(2 minutes active)
SERVINGS 2

INGREDIENTS

- 1 cup dry white wine
- 2 (6-ounce) salmon fillets
- 4 lemon slices
- ½ teaspoon kosher salt
- ½ teaspoon ground black pepper
  Garnishes: lemon slices, dill sprigs

1 In an Instant Pot, add wine. Place steamer inside pot. Place fillets, skin-side down, in steamer. Place 2 lemon slices on each fillet. Season with salt and pepper.
2 Lock lid; set pressure release valve to Sealing. Select Pressure Cook. Select High Pressure; set timer for 6 minutes.
3 When time is up, use quick release. Unlock lid. Place fillets on serving plates; garnish with lemon and dill.

Poached Mahi-Mahi With Butter Sauce

Mahi-mahi lives up to its nickname as "the poor man's lobster" in this decadent preparation.

START TO FINISH 18 minutes
(3 minutes active)
SERVINGS 4

INGREDIENTS

- 1 teaspoon paprika
- ½ teaspoon onion powder
- ½ teaspoon sea salt
- ½ teaspoon ground black pepper
- 4 frozen skinless mahi-mahi fillets
- 8 tablespoons butter, sliced
  Steamed vegetables
  Garnishes: chopped parsley, lemon slices

1 In a bowl, stir together paprika, onion powder, salt and pepper.
2 In an Instant Pot, add 1½ cups water. Place steam rack in pot; place a 7-inch round baking dish on rack. Place fillets in dish; sprinkle with seasoning and top with butter.
3 Lock lid; set pressure release valve to Sealing. Select Pressure Cook. Select High Pressure; set timer for 8 minutes.
4 When time is up, use quick release. Unlock lid.
5 Place fillets and vegetables on serving plates; spoon sauce over top and garnish, as desired.

Shrimp Risotto

Shallots add a milder flavor than onions in this delicate rice dish.

START TO FINISH 30 minutes
(10 minutes active)
SERVINGS 6

INGREDIENTS

- 4 tablespoons butter, divided
- 2 large shallots, chopped
- 1½ cups arborio rice
- 2 cloves garlic, minced
- ½ cup dry white wine
- 4 cups seafood stock
- 1 pound peeled, deveined medium shrimp
- ¼ teaspoon kosher salt
- ¼ teaspoon ground black pepper
- 1 cup frozen peas
- ¼ cup grated Parmesan cheese
  Garnish: chopped chives

1 In an Instant Pot, add 2 tablespoons butter. Select Sauté; add shallots and cook, stirring, 5 minutes. Add rice and garlic. Stir in wine. Cook 1 minute. Add stock.
2 Lock lid; set pressure release valve to Sealing. Select Pressure Cook. Select High Pressure; set timer for 8 minutes.
3 Meanwhile, in a large nonstick skillet over medium heat, melt remaining butter. Add shrimp, salt and pepper; cook 3 minutes. Stir in peas; cook 1 additional minute.
4 When time is up, use natural release. Unlock lid; stir in shrimp, peas and Parmesan.
5 Garnish with chives and serve.

Mussels With White Wine Sauce

Serve with plenty of toasted bread for dipping!

START TO FINISH 30 minutes
(10 minutes active)

SERVINGS 4

INGREDIENTS

- 2 tablespoons olive oil
- 2 tablespoons butter
- 1 shallot, sliced
- 1 teaspoon minced garlic
- 1 cup cherry tomatoes, halved
- 3 thyme sprigs
- $\frac{1}{2}$ teaspoon sea salt
- $\frac{3}{4}$ cup dry white wine
- $\frac{3}{4}$ cup seafood stock
- 2 pounds mussels in the shell, scrubbed
- 1 tablespoon chopped curly parsley
  Sourdough French bread rounds, toasted

1 On an Instant Pot, select Sauté; add oil, butter, shallot and garlic and cook for 3 minutes.

2 Add tomatoes, thyme and salt; cook for 2 additional minutes.

3 Add wine; bring to a simmer and cook for 3 minutes to reduce. Add stock; bring to a simmer again.

4 Add mussels to pot; stir to coat. Select Cancel. Lock lid; set pressure release valve to Sealing. Select Pressure Cook. Select High Pressure; set timer for 2 minutes.

5 When time is up, use quick release; unlock lid. Spoon mussels into a large shallow serving bowl (discard any that did not open during cooking). Pour cooking liquid over top.

6 Sprinkle with parsley; serve with toast rounds.

QUICK TIP

The secret to getting a good sear on scallops is letting them cook without flipping or moving them for 2 or 3 minutes.

Seared Scallops With Risotto

Seared Scallops With Risotto

Golden-brown sea scallops add an elegant touch.

START TO FINISH 35 minutes
(15 minutes active)
SERVINGS 4

INGREDIENTS

- 3 tablespoons olive oil, divided
- 3 tablespoons butter, divided
- 1½ cups sliced leeks
- 1 teaspoon minced garlic
- 1½ cups uncooked arborio rice
- 3 thyme sprigs
- ½ cup dry white wine
- 1 (32-ounce box) chicken broth
- 2 teaspoons kosher salt, divided
- 1 teaspoon black pepper, divided
- 16 sea scallops
- ¾ cup grated Parmesan cheese
- 2 teaspoons lemon juice
  Garnishes: thyme leaves, lemon slices

1 In an Instant Pot, add 2 tablespoons oil and 1 tablespoon butter. Select Sauté; heat until melted.

2 Add leeks; cook about 5 minutes. Add garlic; cook 1 additional minute. Stir in rice; cook 1 minute.

3 Add thyme and wine; cook until slightly reduced, about 3 minutes. Stir in broth, 1 teaspoon salt and ½ teaspoon pepper until combined.

4 Select Cancel; lock lid. Set pressure release valve to Sealing. Select Pressure Cook; set timer for 7 minutes.

5 Meanwhile, use paper towels to pat scallops dry; sprinkle with remaining salt and pepper.

6 In a large skillet over high heat, heat remaining oil. Add scallops; cook, undisturbed, until golden brown, about 2 minutes; flip and cook on other side for 2 minutes.

7 When time is up, use quick release. Unlock lid; stir risotto until creamy. Stir in Parmesan, lemon juice and remaining butter until combined.

8 Divide risotto among 4 serving bowls. Top with scallops; garnish with thyme and lemon slices.

Shrimp & Grits

Shrimp & Grits

This Southern dish is a real treat for breakfast or lunch.

START TO FINISH 35 minutes
(10 minutes active)
SERVINGS 4

INGREDIENTS

- 4 slices bacon, chopped
- 1 onion, chopped
- 1 teaspoon minced garlic
- ½ cup chicken broth
- 1 teaspoon Creole seasoning
- 1 tablespoon lemon juice
- 1 pound raw jumbo shrimp, peeled and deveined, with tails on
- 1 tablespoon Old Bay seasoning
- 2 tablespoons butter
  Hot cooked grits
  Garnish: chopped parsley

1 On an Instant Pot, select Sauté; add bacon, onion and garlic. Cook for 4 minutes.

2 Add broth, Creole seasoning and lemon juice.

3 Stir in shrimp and Old Bay seasoning.

4 Lock lid; set pressure release valve to Sealing. Select Pressure Cook. Select high heat; set timer for 1 minute.

5 When time is up, use quick release. Unlock lid.

6 Stir in butter and serve over grits. Garnish with parsley.

PASTA, RICE, BEANS & GRAINS

~~~~~~~~

YOU'LL FIND INSPIRATION IN THESE
RECIPES, FROM CLASSIC SIDES LIKE PERFECT
RICE TO INNOVATIVE MAINS SUCH AS
BACON PASTA CARBONARA.

Creamy Ziti,
page 78

Homemade
Macaroni
& Cheese

Creamy Ziti

Adding cream to the tomato sauce ensures it will coat the ziti.

START TO FINISH 25 minutes
(10 minutes active)

SERVINGS 4

INGREDIENTS

1¼ cups chicken broth
1 cup heavy cream
2 teaspoons garlic, minced
1 teaspoon kosher salt
½ teaspoon ground black pepper
1 (12-ounce) box dried ziti pasta
1½ cups tomato sauce
1 cup Parmesan cheese, shredded
1 cup mozzarella cheese, shredded
1½ cups fresh spinach, cut into thin shreds
Red pepper flakes

1 In an Instant Pot, layer broth, cream, garlic, salt, pepper and pasta.
2 Lock lid; set pressure release valve to Sealing. Select Pressure Cook. Select High Pressure; set timer for 6 minutes.
3 When time is up, use natural release for 6 minutes, then quick-release remaining pressure. Unlock lid. Stir in tomato sauce.
4 Add cheeses, ⅓ cup at a time, stirring constantly until fully melted.
5 Serve hot, topped with spinach and red pepper flakes.

Homemade Macaroni & Cheese

Put down the boxed version—this Instant Pot recipe is a cinch to make.

START TO FINISH 30 minutes
(25 minutes active)

SERVINGS 6

INGREDIENTS

1 (16-ounce) box elbow macaroni
1 teaspoon salt
½ teaspoon ground black pepper
1 (12-ounce) can evaporated milk
¼ cup butter
¼ cup heavy cream
3 cups shredded sharp cheddar cheese

1 In an Instant Pot, stir macaroni, 4 cups water and salt.
2 Lock lid; set pressure release valve to Sealing. Select Pressure Cook. Select High Pressure; set timer for 4 minutes.
3 When time is up, use quick release. Unlock lid.
4 Select Sauté; stir in evaporated milk, butter and cream. Add cheese, stirring constantly until cheese is completely melted.

QUICK TIP

Try a blend of cheeses in your mac. Some we really love: fontina, Gruyère and smoked Gouda.

3-Cheese Mac With Crispy Browned-Butter Breadcrumbs

Give this cheesy, creamy family favorite a nutritional boost by adding veggies, or spice things up with a flavorful salsa.

START TO FINISH 30 minutes (20 minutes active)

SERVINGS 4

INGREDIENTS

- 2 tablespoons butter, divided
- ¼ cup plain panko breadcrumbs
- 8 ounces dried corkscrew pasta
- 1 small onion, finely chopped
- 3 cloves garlic, minced
- ¼ teaspoon salt
- ½ teaspoon dry mustard
  Pinch cayenne pepper
- 3 cups water
- 1 cup shredded cheddar cheese
- 1 cup shredded fontina cheese
- ½ cup shredded manchego cheese
- 2 ounces cream cheese, cut into cubes
- ¾ cup half-and-half
  Finely chopped parsley

1 On an Instant Pot, select Sauté. Stir in 1 tablespoon butter until golden brown, stirring constantly. Stir in breadcrumbs to coat. Cook breadcrumbs, stirring frequently, until lightly toasted and fragrant.

2 Spread breadcrumbs in a thin layer on a plate. Use a paper towel to wipe out inside of pot.

3 Add pasta, onion, garlic, remaining butter, salt, mustard and cayenne to pot. Pour in water.

4 Lock lid; set pressure release valve to Sealing. Select Pressure Cook. Select High Pressure; set timer for 2 minutes.

5 When time is up, use natural release. Unlock lid (do not drain off liquid). Select Cancel.

6 Add cheddar, fontina and manchego cheeses to pot. Stir in cream cheese and half-and-half. Select Sauté. Cook and stir for 2 to 3 minutes or until cheese is melted and mixture is well combined.

7 Sprinkle with toasted breadcrumbs and parsley to serve.

PEAS & CARROTS 3-CHEESE MAC
Prepare as directed, except add 1 cup frozen (thawed) peas and carrots with pasta.

SALSA 3-CHEESE MAC Prepare as directed, except stir in ¾ cup jarred salsa with cheeses.

Ravioli With Pesto

Ravioli With Pesto

If you don't like mushroom, choose your favorite ravioli filling.

START TO FINISH 20 minutes
(5 minutes active)

SERVINGS 6

INGREDIENTS

 2 (9-ounce) packages refrigerated mushroom and cheese–filled ravioli
 1 (7-ounce) container refrigerated basil pesto
 Garnishes: grated Parmesan cheese, red pepper flakes, pine nuts, basil leaves

1 Pour 3 cups water into an Instant Pot. Select Sauté on High; set timer for 10 minutes.
2 Add ravioli to pot. Press Cancel.
3 Lock lid; set pressure release valve to Sealing. Select Pressure Cook. Select High Pressure; set timer for 3 minutes.
4 When time is up, use quick release. Unlock lid; drain ravioli.
5 Place ravioli in a large bowl; toss with pesto. Garnish, as desired.

Italian Sausage One-Pot Pasta

An Instant Pot allows the flavors to meld and makes cleanup easy.

START TO FINISH 25 minutes
(10 minutes active)

SERVINGS 6

INGREDIENTS

 1 tablespoon olive oil
 1 pound Italian sausage links
 2 (24-ounce) jars tomato-basil pasta sauce
 1 pound penne pasta
 Garnish: basil leaves

1 On an Instant Pot, select Sauté; heat oil. Add sausage; cook for 5 minutes. Remove sausage and slice into rounds.
2 Wipe out excess oil from pot. Add sausage, pasta sauce, 2 cups water and pasta to pot; stir to combine.
3 Lock lid; set pressure release valve to Sealing. Select Pressure Cook.

Select High Pressure; set timer for 8 minutes.
4 When time is up, use natural release for 6 minutes, then quick-release remaining pressure. Unlock lid.
5 Garnish with basil.

Cincinnati Chili Over Spaghetti

The cinnamon and cocoa in this chili dish are surprisingly delicious!

START TO FINISH 25 minutes
(5 minutes active)

SERVINGS 6

INGREDIENTS

 1 tablespoon olive oil
 1 pound ground beef
 1 onion, diced
 1 teaspoon minced garlic
 2 cups beef broth
 2 tablespoons chili powder
 1 tablespoon cumin
 1 teaspoon cinnamon
 1 bay leaf
 1 cup tomato sauce
 1 tablespoon red wine vinegar
 1 tablespoon cocoa powder
 1 teaspoon salt
 1 teaspoon ground black pepper
 Hot cooked spaghetti
 Garnishes: shredded cheddar, chopped onion, oyster crackers

1 Press Sauté; heat oil in Instant Pot. Add beef, onion and garlic; cook for 6 minutes.
2 Drain mixture and return to pot. Add broth, stirring to combine.
3 Add remaining ingredients, except spaghetti, stirring until combined.
4 Lock lid; set pressure release valve to Sealing. Select Pressure Cook. Select High Pressure; set timer for 5 minutes.
5 When time is up, use natural release for 10 minutes, then quick-release remaining pressure. Unlock lid; discard bay leaf.
6 Use an immersion blender for a smooth consistency.
7 Serve over pasta with desired garnishes.

Orzo With Herbs

Pasta Puttanesca

This dish was created to make a fast meal with just basic ingredients.

START TO FINISH 15 minutes (10 minutes active)

SERVINGS 6

INGREDIENTS

- 1 teaspoon minced garlic
- 1 (32-ounce) jar tomato–basil pasta sauce
- 3 cups water
- 4 cups dried penne pasta
- ¼ teaspoon crushed red pepper flakes
- 1 tablespoon drained capers
- ½ cup pitted Kalamata olives (cut some in half)
- 1 teaspoon kosher salt
- ¼ teaspoon ground black pepper
- 1 teaspoon grated lemon zest

1 In an Instant Pot, add all ingredients; stir to coat pasta.
2 Lock lid; set pressure release valve to Sealing. Select Pressure Cook. Select High Pressure; set timer for 5 minutes.
3 When time is up, use quick release. Unlock lid and serve.

Orzo With Herbs

This rice look-alike makes a tasty side for grilled chicken, fish or any main meal recipe.

START TO FINISH 15 minutes (5 minutes active)

SERVINGS 4

INGREDIENTS

- 2½ cups dried orzo pasta
- ½ teaspoon sea salt
- 1 tablespoon chopped parsley
- 1 teaspoon chopped thyme
- 1 teaspoon minced garlic
- 1 teaspoon lemon zest
- 1 cup frozen peas, thawed
- 4 cups vegetable broth
- 2 tablespoons olive oil
- 1 tablespoon chopped basil leaves
  Garnish: basil leaves

1 In an Instant Pot, add all ingredients except basil. Stir well to mix.
2 Lock lid; set pressure release valve to Sealing. Select Pressure Cook. Select High Pressure; set timer for 5 minutes.
3 When time is up, use natural release for 5 minutes, then quick-release remaining pressure. Unlock lid.
4 Stir in chopped basil. Garnish with basil leaves.

Bacon Pasta Carbonara

Bucatini is thicker than spaghetti, with a hole through the center to pick up even more of the decadent sauce. Try pancetta instead of bacon for a tasty variation.

START TO FINISH 25 minutes (10 minutes active)

SERVINGS 6

INGREDIENTS

- 6 slices bacon, chopped
- 1 teaspoon minced garlic
- 1 small onion, chopped
- 1 (16-ounce) package bucatini
- 3 eggs
- ⅓ cup heavy cream
- ½ pound grated Parmesan cheese, divided

Garnishes: cracked pepper, chopped parsley

1 On an Instant Pot, select Sauté; add bacon and cook until golden, about 5 minutes. Remove from pot; crumble and set aside.

2 Add garlic and onion to pot; cook 1 minute.

3 Pour in 4 cups water; add pasta.

4 Lock lid; set pressure release valve to Sealing. Select Pressure Cook. Select High Pressure; set timer for 5 minutes.

5 Meanwhile, in a bowl, mix eggs, cream and ¼ pound cheese.

6 When time is up, use quick release. Unlock lid.

7 Stir in egg mixture until pasta is well coated.

8 Serve with remaining cheese and crumbled bacon.

9 Garnish, as desired.

Vegetable Lo Mein

Lo mein noodles can be found in many large grocery stores, or substitute with fettuccine (as shown).

START TO FINISH 20 minutes
(10 minutes active)

SERVINGS 4

INGREDIENTS

- 1 tablespoon dark sesame oil
- 1 teaspoon chopped garlic
- 1 teaspoon chopped ginger
- 1 (8-ounce) package lo mein noodles, broken in half
- 1 cup trimmed sugar snap peas
- 1 cup broccoli florets
- 2 carrots, cut into matchsticks
- 3 scallions, sliced
- 1½ cups vegetable broth
- 2 tablespoons soy sauce
- 1 tablespoon oyster sauce
- 1 tablespoon rice vinegar
- 1 tablespoon dark brown sugar
  Garnishes: sliced scallions, red pepper flakes

1 On an Instant Pot, select Sauté; heat oil. Add garlic and ginger; stir for 1 minute.

2 Spread noodles in pot. Add vegetables on top of noodles.

3 In a medium bowl, mix broth, soy sauce, oyster sauce, rice vinegar and sugar. Pour over vegetables.

4 Lock lid; set pressure release valve to Sealing. Select Pressure Cook. Select High Pressure; set timer for 5 minutes.

5 When time is up, use quick release. Unlock lid.

6 Stir the noodles and serve, garnished with scallions and red pepper flakes.

Pad Thai With Vegetables

Pad Thai With Vegetables

This dish is traditionally made with flat rice noodles, but we love the texture of spaghetti in this version. Stir in cubes of firm tofu if you want to add some vegetarian protein. You can also select a whole-wheat pasta for additional fiber and protein.

START TO FINISH: 25 minutes

(10 minutes active)

SERVINGS 2

INGREDIENTS

- 2 tablespoons vegetable oil
- 1 teaspoon chopped garlic
- 1 teaspoon minced ginger
- 1 red bell pepper, sliced
- 3 scallions, sliced
- 3 tablespoons soy sauce
- 2 tablespoons rice vinegar
- 2 tablespoons honey
- 1 tablespoon Sriracha sauce
- 3 tablespoons creamy peanut butter
- $^{1}/_{2}$ teaspoon salt
- 1 (8-ounce) package spaghetti, broken into half
- $1^{1}/_{2}$ cups water or vegetable broth
- 2 tablespoons chopped fresh cilantro
- 3 tablespoons fresh lime juice Garnishes: chopped peanuts, lime wedges

1 On an Instant Pot, select Sauté; heat oil. Cook garlic and ginger for 1 minute. Stir in bell pepper and scallions. Stir in soy sauce, rice vinegar, honey, Sriracha, peanut butter and salt.

2 Add spaghetti to pot and stir; add water or vegetable broth.

3 Lock lid; set pressure release valve to Sealing. Select Pressure Cook. Select High Pressure; set timer for 4 minutes.

4 When time is up, use quick release. Unlock lid.

5 Stir the noodle mixture together. Add cilantro and lime juice.

6 Top with desired garnishes and serve immediately.

Perfect Rice

You'll reach for this recipe often as you make the dishes in this book.

START TO FINISH 20 minutes

(1 minute active)

SERVINGS 4

INGREDIENTS

- 1 cup white rice
- 1 cup water
- $^{1}/_{2}$ teaspoon salt Cracked black pepper Butter

1 Place all ingredients in Instant Pot.

2 Lock lid; set pressure release valve to Sealing. Select Pressure Cook. Select High Pressure; set timer for 3 minutes.

3 When time is up, use natural release for 20 minutes, then quick-release remaining pressure. Unlock lid.

4 Remove rice from Instant Pot. Use in one of our recipes, or serve with cracked pepper and butter.

Mushroom Risotto

1 On an Instant Pot, select Sauté; heat oil. Add onion and rice. Cook and stir for 5 minutes or until rice looks translucent. Stir in wine; cook and stir for 2 to 3 minutes or until wine is absorbed. Select Cancel.

2 Add salt, pepper, broth and saffron.

3 Lock lid; set pressure release valve to Sealing. Select Pressure Cook. Select High Pressure; set timer for 8 minutes.

4 When time is up, use quick release. Unlock lid.

5 Stir until any surface liquid is gone; stir in butter and cheese. Let stand for 5 to 10 minutes before serving.

Mushroom Risotto

The flavor of the mushrooms permeates the risotto, making this dish delicious when served all on its own or as a side.

START TO FINISH 25 minutes
(15 minutes active)

SERVINGS 4

INGREDIENTS

- 2 tablespoons olive oil
- 1 small onion, diced
- 1 teaspoon minced garlic
- 1 (8-ounce) package sliced cremini mushrooms
- 1½ cups arborio rice
- 2 teaspoons salt
- ½ teaspoon ground black pepper
- 2½ cups chicken stock
- 2 tablespoons butter
  Garnish: fresh thyme

1 On an Instant Pot, select Sauté; heat oil. Add onion and cook for 5 minutes. Stir in garlic and mushrooms; cook for 3 minutes.

2 Add rice, salt and pepper; cook another minute. Select Cancel.

3 Add stock to pot. Lock lid; set pressure release valve to Sealing. Select Pressure Cook. Select High Pressure; set timer for 10 minutes.

4 When time is up, use quick release. Unlock lid. Stir in butter until melted.

5 Garnish with fresh thyme.

Creamy Risotto With Parmesan & Herbs

Once you make risotto in an Instant Pot, you'll be hooked! And you won't miss having to constantly stir the pot.

START TO FINISH 25 minutes
(5 minutes active)

SERVINGS 4

INGREDIENTS

- ¼ cup butter
- 1 onion, chopped
- 1 teaspoon minced garlic
- 1½ cups arborio rice
- 4 cups chicken broth, divided
- ¼ cup grated Parmesan cheese
- ½ teaspoon salt
- ½ teaspoon ground black pepper
  Garnishes: grated Parmesan, chopped parsley, thyme sprigs

1 On an Instant Pot, select Sauté; melt butter. Add onion; cook for 5 minutes. Stir in garlic and rice; cook 1 more minute. Stir in 1 cup broth; cook 2 more minutes.

2 Add remaining broth, Parmesan cheese, salt and pepper.

3 Lock lid; set pressure release valve to Sealing. Select Pressure Cook.

Select High Pressure; set timer for 10 minutes.

4 When time is up, use natural release for 10 minutes, then quick-release remaining pressure. Unlock lid.

5 Spoon into serving bowls and top with garnishes, as desired.

Saffron Risotto

Saffron is one of the world's priciest spices, but it adds a subtle flavor and a bright yellow hue to the rice.

START TO FINISH 30 minutes
(15 minutes active)

SERVINGS 6

INGREDIENTS

- 2 tablespoons olive oil
- 1 small yellow onion, finely chopped
- 1½ cups arborio rice
- 1 cup dry white wine
- ½ teaspoon salt
- ¼ teaspoon freshly ground black pepper
- 5 cups chicken broth
- 2 pinches saffron threads
- 1 tablespoon butter
- ½ cup grated Parmesan cheese

Lemony Risotto With Peas

The Instant Pot takes the labor out of this often intensive dish.

START TO FINISH 20 minutes (5 minutes active)

SERVINGS 6

INGREDIENTS

- 1 tablespoon olive oil
- 1 cup chopped leeks
- 2 cups arborio rice, rinsed
- ¼ cup dry white wine
- 5 cups chicken broth, divided
- 1½ teaspoons kosher salt
- ½ teaspoon ground black pepper
- ⅓ cup grated Parmesan cheese
- 1 teaspoon lemon zest
- 1 teaspoon chopped thyme
- 1 tablespoon chopped parsley
- 1 cup frozen peas, thawed
- 2 tablespoons butter
  Garnishes: chopped parsley, thyme sprigs, lemon wedges

1 On an Instant Pot, select Sauté. Heat olive oil; add leeks. Cook 5 minutes, stirring often. Add rice and cook, stirring constantly, for 2 minutes.

2 Add wine and cook for 1 minute. Stir in 4 cups broth, salt and pepper.

3 Select Cancel. Lock lid; set pressure release valve to Sealing. Select Pressure Cook. Select High Pressure; set timer for 5 minutes.

4 When time is up, use natural release for 5 minutes, then quick-release remaining pressure. Unlock lid.

5 Stir in remaining broth, Parmesan, lemon zest, herbs, peas and butter. Serve hot and garnish, as desired.

Green Rice

Parsley and cilantro give this rice a gorgeous color and a fresh taste.

START TO FINISH 30 minutes
(10 minutes active)

SERVINGS 4

INGREDIENTS

- ½ cup fresh parsley
- ½ cup fresh cilantro
- 1 poblano pepper, roughly chopped
- ¼ cup chopped yellow onion
- 1 cup chicken broth, divided
- 1 cup jasmine rice, rinsed
- 1 teaspoon kosher salt
- ½ teaspoon ground black pepper
- 2 teaspoons olive oil
  Garnish: cilantro leaves

1 In the bowl of a food processor, combine parsley, cilantro, poblano, onion and ½ cup chicken broth. Process until finely chopped, about 20 seconds.

2 In an Instant Pot, add herb mixture, remaining broth, rice, salt, pepper and oil, stirring to submerge rice completely in liquid.

3 Lock lid; select Rice. Set pressure release valve to Sealing.

4 When time is up, use natural release for 10 minutes, then quick-release remaining pressure. Unlock lid. Fluff rice with a fork. Garnish with cilantro leaves.

Cheesy Broccoli & Rice

Make this a meal by adding in some leftover roast chicken.

START TO FINISH 16 minutes
(5 minutes active)

SERVINGS 6

INGREDIENTS

- 1 tablespoon butter
- ¹/₂ cup diced onion
- 1 teaspoon minced garlic
- 2¹/₂ cups chicken broth, divided
- 1 cup medium-grain white rice
- 2 cups chopped broccoli florets
- ¹/₂ teaspoon kosher salt
- ¹/₂ teaspoon ground black pepper
- 1 cup shredded sharp cheddar cheese, plus extra for garnish

1 On an Instant Pot, select Sauté. Add butter and onion; cook until soft, about 3 to 5 minutes. Add garlic; cook, stirring constantly, about 30 seconds. Select Cancel.
2 Pour in 2 cups broth and rice; stir. Lock lid; set pressure release valve to Sealing. Select Pressure Cook. Select High Pressure; set timer for 5 minutes.
3 When time is up, use quick release. Unlock lid.
4 Stir in broccoli, remaining broth, and salt and pepper.
5 Lock lid; set pressure release valve to Sealing. Select Pressure Cook. Select High Pressure; set timer for 1 minute.
6 When time is up, use quick release. Unlock lid.
7 Stir in cheese until melted and creamy. Sprinkle with additional shredded cheese to serve.

Cuban Black Beans & Rice

Rice and beans are a classic combo that offer a complete array of proteins.

START TO FINISH 30 minutes
(10 minutes active)

SERVINGS 4

INGREDIENTS

- 2 tablespoons vegetable oil
- 1 onion, finely chopped

Cheesy Broccoli & Rice

- 1 green bell pepper, chopped
- 1 jalapeño, seeded and chopped
- 2 cloves garlic, minced
- 1 cup long-grain white rice
- 1 tablespoon chicken-flavor soup base
- 1³/₄ cups warm water
- 1 (15-ounce) can black beans, undrained
- 1 whole bay leaf
- ¹/₄ teaspoon ground cumin
- ¹/₂ teaspoon smoked paprika
     Salt
- ¹/₄ cup chopped fresh cilantro
     Lime wedges

1 On an Instant Pot, select Sauté; heat vegetable oil. Add onion, green bell pepper, jalapeño and garlic. Cook and stir until vegetables are softened, about 3 to 5 minutes. Add rice; stir for 2 minutes. Select Cancel.
2 In a mixing cup, stir together soup base and water. Add soup base, beans, bay leaf, cumin and paprika to pot.
3 Lock lid; set pressure release valve to Sealing. Select Pressure Cook. Select High Pressure; set timer for 8 minutes.
4 When time is up, use natural release. Unlock lid. Season to taste

with salt. Sprinkle with cilantro and serve lime wedges on the side.

Coconut Rice

This pairs particularly well with Thai and Indian dishes, and it's also yummy as the base of a veggie bowl.

START TO FINISH 25 minutes
(5 minutes active)

SERVINGS 4

INGREDIENTS

- 1¹/₂ cups jasmine rice, rinsed
- 1 (13.5-ounce) can unsweetened coconut milk
- 2 teaspoons olive oil
- 1 teaspoon kosher salt
- 1 teaspoon sugar
     Garnishes: sliced scallions, toasted coconut flakes

1 In an Instant Pot, add all ingredients, stirring to submerge rice completely in liquid. Lock lid; select Rice. Set pressure release valve to Sealing.
2 When time is up, use natural release for 10 minutes, then quick-release remaining pressure. Remove lid.
3 Fluff rice with a fork. Top with scallions and coconut flakes; serve immediately.

Thai Green
Curry Tofu

Thai Green Curry Tofu

Eliminate the fish sauce to turn this
into a vegan-friendly main meal.

START TO FINISH 35 minutes
(15 minutes active)

SERVINGS 4

INGREDIENTS

  1 tablespoon coconut oil
  1 shallot, thinly sliced
  1 tablespoon minced fresh ginger
  1 serrano pepper, seeded
     and minced
 ½ teaspoon salt
  1 (14-ounce) can coconut milk,
     shaken
  2 teaspoons fish sauce
  1 teaspoon sugar
 ¼ cup Thai green curry paste
  2 carrots, thinly sliced
  8 ounces fresh snow peas,
     trimmed
  1 medium yellow or red sweet
     pepper, cut into strips
  1 (8-ounce) block extra-firm tofu,
     cut into ¾-inch cubes

     Hot cooked jasmine rice
 ¼ cup chopped fresh cilantro leaves
 ¼ cup thinly sliced fresh basil
     leaves
  4 lime wedges

1 On an Instant Pot, select Sauté; heat
oil. Add shallot, ginger and serrano
pepper; cook, stirring, until slightly
wilted, about 2 minutes. Add salt.
Select Cancel.
2 Stir in coconut milk, fish sauce,
sugar and curry paste. Stir in carrots,
snow peas, sweet pepper and tofu.
3 Lock lid; set pressure release valve
to Sealing. Select Pressure Cook.
Select High Pressure; set timer for
3 minutes. When time is up, use
quick release. Unlock lid.
4 Serve over rice; sprinkle with
cilantro and basil. Add a lime wedge
to each serving.

Quinoa With Toppings

This healthy seed has a nutty
flavor and is loaded with protein.
Our version has a Mexican flair;
personalize your toppings to suit
your taste.

START TO FINISH 30 minutes
(15 minutes active)

SERVINGS 4

INGREDIENTS

  1 cup uncooked red and white
     quinoa, rinsed and drained
1¼ cups water or broth
 ½ teaspoon salt
 ½ teaspoon ground black pepper
     Toppings: red beans, cilantro,
     sliced avocado, cherry tomatoes

1 In an Instant Pot, stir quinoa and
water or broth.
2 Lock lid; set pressure release valve
to Sealing. Select Pressure Cook.
Select High Pressure; set timer for
1 minute.
3 When time is up, use natural
release for 10 minutes, then quick-
release remaining pressure.
4 Unlock lid. Fluff quinoa with a
fork. Season with salt and pepper.
5 Serve with toppings on the side,
or try different toppings.

Quinoa With Toppings

SOUPS & STEWS

DINNER HAS NEVER BEEN EASIER, THANKS TO THESE WARM, HEARTY AND FILLING MEALS IN A BOWL.

Brunswick Stew,
page 100

Shrimp & Rice Stew

1 pound large shrimp, peeled and deveined

1 pound cod or other whitefish, cut into 1-inch pieces

1 pound mussels, cleaned and steamed

1 On an Instant Pot, select Sauté; heat oil. Add onion and next 4 ingredients, cook until soft, about 3 minutes.
2 Add all remaining ingredients except mussels. Lock lid; set pressure release valve to Sealing. Select Pressure Cook. Select High Pressure; set timer for 7 minutes.
3 When time is up, use natural release for 10 minutes, then quick-release remaining pressure. Unlock lid. Stir in mussels to heat.

Creamy Butternut Soup

Save prep time by purchasing precut butternut squash, readily available at many grocery stores.

START TO FINISH 30 minutes
(10 minutes active)

SERVINGS 4–6

INGREDIENTS

1 medium onion, chopped

2 pounds butternut squash, peeled, halved and seeds removed, cut into chunks

2 (15-ounce) cans chicken broth

½ cup Madeira, sherry or Marsala

½ teaspoon nutmeg

3 cloves garlic

1 cup sour cream
Snipped fresh sage

1 In an Instant Pot, add onion, squash, broth, wine, nutmeg and garlic.
2 Lock lid; set pressure release valve to Sealing. Select Pressure Cook. Select High Pressure; set timer for 6 minutes.
3 When time is up, use quick release. Unlock lid. Stir in sour cream.
4 Use an immersion blender (or regular blender) to puree soup.
5 If necessary, warm soup in the Instant Pot (adjusted to low/less).
6 Serve in rustic bowls, topped with snipped fresh sage.

Shrimp & Rice Stew

You'll love the flavors Old Bay seasoning adds to this delicious stew.

START TO FINISH 25 minutes
(10 minutes active)

SERVINGS 4

INGREDIENTS

2 tablespoons olive oil

1 onion, sliced

1 teaspoon chopped garlic

1 teaspoon salt

1 teaspoon ground black pepper

2 teaspoons paprika

2 bay leaves

1½ cups chopped tomatoes

2 cups seafood stock

1 teaspoon Old Bay seasoning

2 pounds large shrimp, peeled and deveined

1 cup rice, drained and rinsed
Garnish: scallion slices

1 On an Instant Pot, select Sauté; heat oil. Stir in onion, garlic, salt, pepper and paprika.
2 Stir in bay leaves, tomatoes, stock and Old Bay seasoning; cook 1 minute.
3 Stir in shrimp and rice.
4 Lock lid; set pressure release valve to Sealing. Select Pressure Cook. Select High Pressure; set timer for 12 minutes.
5 When time is up, use quick release. Unlock lid. Sprinkle with scallions.

Seafood Cioppino

This stew was originally made with the catch of the day, so add whatever fish or shellfish you like! Serve this with thick slices of crusty bread.

START TO FINISH 25 minutes
(5 minutes active)

SERVINGS 4

INGREDIENTS

1 tablespoon vegetable oil

1 onion, diced

2 carrots, diced

2 stalks celery, diced

1 teaspoon minced garlic

1 leek, cleaned and chopped

½ cup dry white wine

¼ cup lemon juice

3 cups tomato sauce

2 cups vegetable or seafood stock

Creamy
Butternut
Soup

Santa Fe Soup

Santa Fe Soup

Somewhere between soup and a stew, this dish is like a taco in a bowl. You can also sub ground turkey for beef.

START TO FINISH 30 minutes
(15 minutes active)

SERVINGS 8

INGREDIENTS

Vegetable cooking spray
2 pounds lean ground beef
1 onion, chopped
1 packet ranch dressing mix
1 packet taco seasoning mix
1 teaspoon ground black pepper
1 (10-ounce) bag frozen corn
1 (10.5-ounce) can diced tomatoes with chilies
1 (14.5-ounce) can diced tomatoes
1 (14.5-ounce) can white Northern beans, drained and rinsed
1 (14.5-ounce) can light kidney beans, drained and rinsed
1 (14.5-ounce) can black beans, drained and rinsed
1 (14.5-ounce) can chicken broth
Garnishes: sour cream, shredded cheese, cilantro leaves

1 Spray inside of an Instant Pot with vegetable cooking spray.
2 Select Sauté; add ground beef and onion. Cook until beef is no longer pink, about 8 minutes. Drain grease.
3 Stir in all remaining ingredients.
4 Lock lid; set pressure release valve to Sealing. Select Pressure Cook. Select High Pressure; set timer for 10 minutes.
5 When time is up, use natural release for 10 minutes, then quick-release remaining pressure. Unlock lid.
6 Top with desired garnishes.

Beef Vegetable Soup

Often called "hamburger soup," this dish is a family favorite. Serve it with toasted slices of crusty Italian bread on the side for dipping and a green salad—you don't need more than that to make a hearty meal with this dish.

START TO FINISH 30 minutes
(10 minutes active)

SERVINGS 4

INGREDIENTS

1 tablespoon olive oil
1 pound ground beef
1 onion, chopped
2 teaspoons minced garlic
3 tablespoons tomato paste
1 tablespoon Worcestershire sauce
2 bay leaves
2 carrots, peeled and sliced
2 cups beef broth
1 (14.5-ounce) can diced tomatoes
1 cup frozen peas
1 cup frozen corn
1 cup frozen lima beans
1 tablespoon red wine vinegar
Garnish: chopped parsley

1 On an Instant Pot, select Sauté; heat oil. Add ground beef and cook for 5 minutes. Add onion and garlic and cook for 2 minutes.
2 Stir in tomato paste, Worcestershire sauce, bay leaves, carrots, broth and tomatoes.
3 Lock lid; set pressure release valve to Sealing. Select Pressure Cook. Select High Pressure; set timer for 15 minutes.
4 When time is up, use natural release for 10 minutes, then quick-release remaining pressure. Unlock lid.
5 Stir in frozen vegetables until heated through.
6 Garnish with parsley.

QUICK TIP

Check your freezer before buying frozen vegetables—you may have partial bags or cartons in there already, and they're perfect for your Instant Pot soups! Just make sure the amounts you're adding are close to what the recipe calls for.

Brunswick Stew

This hearty, meaty classic will feed a crowd! Use precooked pulled pork or, if time permits, make your own in the Instant Pot and use the leftovers here.

START TO FINISH 30 minutes
(10 minutes active)

SERVINGS 8

INGREDIENTS

- 2 tablespoons vegetable oil
- 1 onion, chopped
- 2 pounds boneless, skinless chicken thighs
- 2 cups chicken stock
- 1 (28-ounce) crushed tomatoes
- 1 teaspoon salt
- 1 teaspoon ground black pepper
- 1 teaspoon hot sauce
- 2 cups frozen butter beans
- 2 cups frozen baby lima beans
- 2 medium potatoes, peeled and chopped
- 1 (15-ounce) can creamed corn
- 1 pound precooked pulled pork (such as Jack Daniel's Seasoned and Cooked Pulled Pork)

1 On an Instant Pot, select Sauté; heat oil. Add onion and cook for 3 minutes.

2 Add chicken; pour in stock. Add tomatoes, salt, pepper and hot sauce.

3 Lock lid; set pressure release valve to Sealing. Select Pressure Cook. Select High Pressure; set timer for 8 minutes.

4 When time is up, use natural release for 5 minutes, then quick-release remaining pressure. Unlock lid.

5 Remove chicken from pot; shred with 2 forks, then return to pot. Stir in remaining ingredients.

6 Lock lid; set pressure release valve to Sealing. Select Pressure Cook. Select High Pressure; set timer for 4 minutes.

7 When time is up, use natural release for 5 minutes, then quick-release remaining pressure. Unlock lid and ladle into bowls.

Red Miso Shrimp Bisque

Red miso (you'll find it in Asian food shops and some grocery stores) adds tons of umami to this soup.

START TO FINISH 25 minutes (10 minutes active)

SERVINGS 4

INGREDIENTS

- 1 tablespoon butter
- 1 pound large shrimp, peeled and deveined, tails on
- 1 teaspoon salt
- ½ teaspoon ground black pepper
- 1 tablespoon olive oil
- 1 cup chopped onion
- ½ cup chopped celery
- 1 cup chopped carrots
- 2 teaspoons chopped garlic
- 2 tablespoons red miso paste
- 2 tablespoons dry sherry
- 1½ cups seafood broth
- 1 (28-ounce) can diced tomatoes
- ½ cup heavy cream
- Garnish: red pepper flakes

1 On an Instant Pot, select Sauté; melt butter.

2 Add shrimp; sprinkle with salt and pepper. Cook shrimp for about 3 minutes or until opaque. Remove; set aside and keep warm.

3 Add oil to pot; heat, then stir in onion, celery, carrots and garlic. Cook for 2 minutes.

4 Stir in miso and sherry to dissolve miso. Stir in broth and tomatoes.

5 Lock lid; set pressure release valve to Sealing. Select Pressure Cook. Select High Pressure; set timer for 8 minutes.

6 When time is up, use quick release. Unlock lid.

7 Stir in cream and serve. Top with shrimp and red pepper flakes.

Borscht

This classic vegetable soup can be served hot or chilled.

START TO FINISH 30 minutes
(15 minutes active)
SERVINGS 4

INGREDIENTS

- 2 tablespoons olive oil
- 1 onion, chopped
- 1 teaspoon salt
- ½ teaspoon ground black pepper
- 2 large russet potatoes, peeled and diced
- 2 large carrots, chopped
- 2 beets, grated
- 1 cup shredded white cabbage
- 2 teaspoons minced garlic
- 3 tablespoons red wine vinegar
- 2 tablespoons tomato paste
- 4 cups vegetable broth

1 On an Instant Pot, select Sauté; heat oil. Add onion, salt and pepper and cook for 2 minutes. Add potatoes and next 7 ingredients.

2 Lock lid; set pressure release valve to Sealing. Select Pressure Cook. Select High Pressure; set timer for 10 minutes.

3 When time is up, use natural release for 10 minutes, then quick-release remaining pressure. Unlock lid and serve.

Sausage-Gnocchi Soup

This hearty soup is perfect served with garlic bread on the side.

START TO FINISH 30 minutes
(5 minutes active)
SERVINGS 4

INGREDIENTS

- 1 pound hot Italian sausage (removed from casings)
- 1 onion, chopped
- 1 teaspoon minced garlic
- 1 teaspoon salt
- ½ teaspoon ground black pepper
- 4¼ cups chicken broth, divided
- 4 cups chopped spinach
- 1 (16-ounce) package gnocchi
- 1½ cups heavy cream
- ¼ cup cornstarch

1 On an Instant Pot, select Sauté. Add sausage; use wooden spoon to break up into bite-size pieces. Add onion and next 3 ingredients.

2 Cook for about 5 minutes to brown sausage. Stir in 4 cups broth.

3 Lock lid; set pressure release valve to Sealing. Select Pressure Cook. Select High Pressure; set timer for 10 minutes.

4 When time is up, use natural release for 10 minutes, then quick-release remaining pressure. Unlock lid.

5 Select Sauté; add spinach, gnocchi and cream.

6 In a small bowl, mix cornstarch and remaining broth. Add to pot and stir until thickened, about 4 minutes.

Quick Chicken Stew

This warming dish cooks in a flash but tastes like it simmered for hours.

START TO FINISH 25 minutes
(10 minutes active)
SERVINGS 4

INGREDIENTS

- 1 pound chicken breasts, cubed
- 2 cups chicken broth
- 1 onion, chopped
- 1 pound baby red potatoes, quartered
- 2 carrots, sliced
- 2 celery stalks, sliced
- ¼ cup chopped parsley
- 1 teaspoon salt
- 1 teaspoon ground black pepper
  Garnishes: cracked black pepper, hot sauce

1 In an Instant Pot, mix all ingredients.

2 Lock lid; set pressure release valve to Sealing. Select Pressure Cook. Select High Pressure; set timer for 10 minutes.

3 When time is up, use natural release for 10 minutes, then quick-release remaining pressure. Unlock lid.

4 Garnish, as desired.

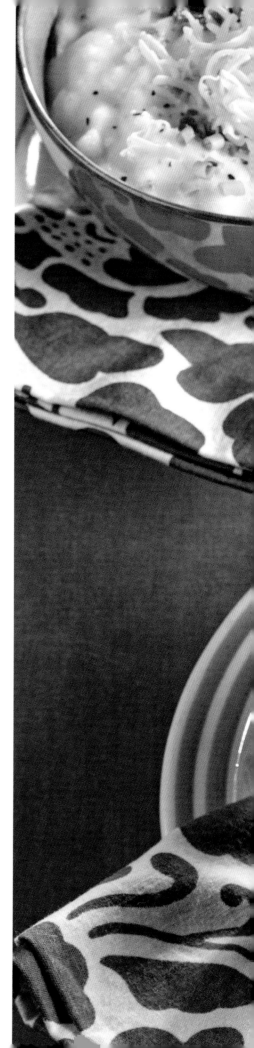

Baked Potato Soup

Be sure to serve extra toppings with this flavorful soup!

START TO FINISH 25 minutes
(15 minutes active)

SERVINGS 6

INGREDIENTS

- 1½ pounds russet potatoes
- 4 tablespoons butter
- ¼ cup flour
- ¾ teaspoon salt
- ½ teaspoon ground black pepper
- 4 cups whole milk
- 1 teaspoon chicken base
- ½ cup sour cream
- ½ cup grated sharp cheddar
- 3 scallions, sliced
- ½ cup cooked, crumbled bacon

1 In an Instant Pot, place steam rack; add 1½ cups water. Place potatoes on rack.

2 Lock lid; set pressure release valve to Sealing. Select Pressure Cook. Select High Pressure; set timer for 20 minutes.

3 When time is up, use natural release. Unlock lid.

4 Place potatoes in large bowl; discard water from pot. Using a potato masher, mash to desired consistency.

5 Select Sauté. Add butter and flour, 1 tablespoon at a time, to pot; whisk until smooth. Stir in salt and pepper.

6 When mixture is bubbling, whisk in milk and chicken base.

7 Adjust heat to High setting. Continue whisking until mixture thickens and bubbles. Stir in potatoes.

8 Divide evenly between 6 serving bowls; top with sour cream, grated sharp cheddar cheese, scallions and bacon to serve.

Tomato
Basil Soup

Tomato Basil Soup

Serve this soup with its BFF:
a grilled cheese sandwich.

START TO FINISH 30 minutes
(10 minutes active)

SERVINGS 4

INGREDIENTS

- 1 tablespoon olive oil
- 1/2 cup diced onion
- 1/2 cup sliced celery
- 1 cup sliced carrots
- 3 cloves garlic, peeled
- 1 tablespoon chopped oregano
- 1 tablespoon chopped parsley
- 1 tablespoon chopped basil
- 1 (28-ounce) can whole peeled tomatoes, undrained
- 1 1/2 cups chicken broth
- 1 teaspoon kosher salt
- 1/4 teaspoon ground black pepper
  Garnishes: basil leaves, oregano leaves

1 On an Instant Pot, select Sauté. Add oil, onion, celery, carrots, garlic, oregano, parsley, basil and tomatoes; cook for 1 minute.

2 Stir in broth, salt and pepper.

3 Lock lid; set pressure release valve to Sealing. Select Pressure Cook. Select High Pressure; set timer for 8 minutes.

4 When time is up, use natural release. Unlock lid; using an immersion blender, puree soup.

5 Garnish, as desired.

Taco Soup

Taco Soup

Serve some tortilla chips on the side, or top it with tortilla strips.

START TO FINISH 30 minutes
(10 minutes active)

SERVINGS 6

INGREDIENTS

- 1 tablespoon canola oil
- 1 1/2 pounds ground beef
- 1 cup chopped yellow onion
- 2 tablespoons all-purpose flour
- 1 (1-ounce) packet taco seasoning mix
- 1 tablespoon ranch dressing mix
- 3 cups beef stock
- 1 cup frozen corn kernels
- 1 (17.6-ounce) box crushed tomatoes
- 1 (16-ounce) can kidney beans in chili sauce, drained and rinsed
- 1 (15-ounce) can black beans, drained and rinsed
- 1 cup shredded cheddar cheese
- 1/2 cup sour cream
- 1/4 cup chopped scallions

1 On an Instant Pot, select Sauté; add oil and heat for 2 minutes. Add beef to pot; stir to break up. Cook, stirring occasionally, until browned, about 8 minutes. Add onion; cook, stirring once, until onion starts to soften, about 6 minutes. Stir in flour, taco season and ranch mix; cook, stirring occasionally, for 2 minutes.

2 Stir in stock, corn, tomatoes and beans.

3 Lock lid; set pressure release valve to Sealing. Select Pressure Cook. Select High Pressure; set timer for 2 minutes.

4 When time is up, use natural release. Unlock lid.

5 Divide soup evenly among 6 serving bowls; top with cheese, sour cream and scallions.

Turkey Potpie Soup

All the goodness of a potpie, but as a soup! Bake your favorite biscuits to top each serving.

START TO FINISH 25 minutes
(5 minutes active)

SERVINGS 8

INGREDIENTS

- 2 tablespoons butter
- 1 onion, chopped
- 1 tablespoon minced garlic
- 3 cups cooked turkey, cut into pieces
- 1 teaspoon salt
- 1/2 teaspoon ground black pepper
- 4 1/4 cups chicken broth, divided
- 3 cups cubed russet potatoes
- 4 slices cooked bacon, crumbled
- 1 (12-ounce) bag frozen mixed vegetables, thawed
- 1 (8-ounce) package cream cheese, softened
- 1/4 cup cornstarch
  Fresh baked biscuits
  Garnish: chopped parsley

1 On an Instant Pot, select Sauté; heat butter. Add onion and garlic and cook for 3 minutes or until softened. Add turkey, salt and pepper. Select Cancel.

2 Pour in 4 cups of broth. Add potatoes and bacon.

3 Lock lid; set pressure release valve to Sealing. Select Pressure Cook. Select High Pressure; set timer for 5 minutes.

4 When time is up, use natural release for 10 minutes, then quick-release remaining pressure. Unlock lid.

5 Select Sauté; stir in vegetables. Add cream cheese and stir until melted.

6 In a small bowl, whisk together cornstarch and remaining broth. Add to soup and cook for an additional 2 to 3 minutes or until thickened.

7 Warm biscuits in a medium oven.

8 Divide soup evenly between bowls; top with biscuits and garnish with parsley.

Tuscan White Bean Soup

If you use dried beans instead of canned, pressure cook for 40 minutes instead of 5. Can't find ground sausage? You can use links instead; just remove them from the casing.

START TO FINISH 40 minutes
(15 minutes active)

SERVINGS 10

INGREDIENTS

- 1 pound ground Italian sausage
- 1 onion, chopped
- 1 teaspoon chopped garlic
- 8 cups chicken broth
- 2 large carrots, sliced
- 1 green bell pepper, chopped
- 3 cans Great Northern beans, drained and rinsed
- 1 tablespoon Italian seasoning
- 2 bay leaves
- 1 (14.5-ounce) can diced tomatoes, undrained
- 4 kale leaves, chopped
  Garnishes: grated Parmesan, thyme sprigs

1 On an Instant Pot, select Sauté; add sausage and cook for 3 minutes, using wooden spoon to break it up.

2 Add onion and garlic; cook for 2 minutes. Pour in broth; use a wooden spoon to scrape up browned bits and deglaze pot.

3 Add carrots, bell pepper, beans, Italian seasoning and bay leaves.

4 Lock lid; set pressure release valve to Sealing. Select Pressure Cook. Select High Pressure; set timer for 5 minutes.

5 When time is up, use natural release for 10 minutes, then quick-release remaining pressure. Unlock lid.

6 Discard bay leaves. Stir in tomatoes and kale.

7 Ladle into bowls and garnish, as desired.

SIDES & SAUCES

SEARCHING FOR WAYS TO ENHANCE YOUR
MAIN DISHES? GET OUT YOUR INSTANT POT,
AND TRY THESE DELECTABLE RECIPES!

Steamed Asparagus
With Hollandaise
Sauce, page 117

Lemony New Potatoes

New potatoes have a waxy texture and keep their shape well in this dish.

START TO FINISH 30 minutes
(10 minutes active)

SERVINGS 6

INGREDIENTS

2 tablespoons extra-virgin olive oil

2 pounds red and purple new potatoes, quartered
1 teaspoon minced garlic
2 teaspoons Greek seasoning
¼ cup fresh lemon juice
½ cup water
   Garnishes: thyme sprigs, seared lemon slices and halves

1 On an Instant Pot, select Sauté; heat oil. Add potatoes and brown on all sides for 3 minutes. Sprinkle with garlic, Greek seasoning, lemon juice and water.

2 Lock lid; set pressure release valve to Sealing. Select Pressure Cook. Select High Pressure; set timer for 7 minutes.

3 When time is up, use natural release for 5 minutes, then quick-release remaining pressure. Unlock lid.

4 Garnish with fresh thyme sprigs and seared lemon slices and halves.

Crispy Green Beans

Crispy Green Beans

Green beans cook to perfection in the Instant Pot. For a softer option, cook an additional 2 minutes.

START TO FINISH 15 minutes
(5 minutes active)

SERVINGS 4

INGREDIENTS

1½ cups chicken broth
2 tablespoons butter
2 pounds green beans, washed and trimmed
½ teaspoon salt
½ teaspoon ground black pepper

1 In an Instant Pot, add broth and butter. Place beans in steamer basket; place in pot. Season with salt and pepper.
2 Lock lid; set pressure release valve to Sealing. Select Pressure Cook. Select High Pressure; set timer for 1 minute.
3 When time is up, use quick release. Unlock lid and serve.

German Potato Salad

This flavorful vinegar-based potato salad makes a nice change from the usual mayo-based ones. Serve it warm alongside steak, pork chops or chicken.

START TO FINISH 30 minutes
(10 minutes active)

SERVINGS 6

INGREDIENTS

6 pieces bacon, chopped
1 onion, chopped
2 pounds small red potatoes, quartered
½ cup chicken broth
½ cup apple cider vinegar
2 tablespoons sugar
1 tablespoon Dijon mustard
1 teaspoon salt
1 teaspoon ground black pepper
Garnish: chopped parsley

1 On an Instant Pot, select Sauté; add bacon and cook until crisp, about 6 minutes. Remove bacon to a paper-towel-lined plate and set aside.
2 Add onion to pot and sauté for 2 minutes. Add bacon back to pot. Add potatoes.
3 In a small bowl, combine broth and remaining ingredients. Pour over potato mixture.
4 Lock lid; set pressure release valve to Sealing. Select Pressure Cook. Select High Pressure; set timer for 6 minutes.
5 When time is up, use quick release. Unlock lid.
6 Place potatoes in serving bowl and garnish with chopped parsley.

Green Beans With
Bacon & Shallots

from the pot using the handles. Rinse beans briefly under cold running water; drain and set aside.

4 Dry inner pot and replace in Instant Pot; coat with cooking spray. Add bacon. Select Sauté; cook 2 minutes. Add shallots; cook, stirring constantly, until shallots are tender and bacon is crisp. Select Cancel.

5 Using a slotted spoon, remove bacon mixture from pot; place in a small bowl, reserving 2 tablespoons of bacon drippings in the pot. Return green beans and bacon mixture to pot; add salt and pepper. Select Sauté; cook, stirring, until thoroughly heated. Serve immediately.

Mashed Cauliflower

This creamy side is a nice change from the usual potatoes. Adjust the amount of broth used for a thinner or thicker mash.

START TO FINISH 20 minutes
(10 minutes active)
SERVINGS 4

INGREDIENTS

- 1 cup vegetable broth
- 1 head cauliflower, cut into large chunks
- $^1/_2$ cup half-and-half
- 3 tablespoons butter
- 1 teaspoon flaky sea salt
- $^1/_2$ teaspoon ground black pepper
  Garnish: chopped chives

1 In an Instant Pot, place a steam rack; pour in broth and place cauliflower on rack.

2 Lock lid; set pressure release valve to Sealing. Select Pressure Cook. Select High Pressure; set timer for 4 minutes.

3 When time is up, use quick release. Unlock lid.

4 In a blender or food processor, place cauliflower and about one-third of broth from pot. Pulse, then blend until smooth.

5 Add half-and-half, butter, salt and pepper; pulse and blend again until totally smooth. Garnish with chopped chives.

Green Beans With Bacon & Shallots

It's amazing what a little bit of bacon can do when you're trying to get kids to eat green veggies!

START TO FINISH 15 minutes
(10 minutes active)
SERVINGS 4

INGREDIENTS

- $1^1/_2$ pounds fresh green beans, trimmed
  Vegetable cooking spray
- 3 bacon slices, cut into $^1/_4$-inch pieces
- $^1/_3$ cup minced shallots
- $^1/_2$ teaspoon sea salt
- $^1/_4$ teaspoon ground black pepper

1 In inner pot of an Instant Pot, pour 1 cup water. Place steam rack in pot, with handles up. Place beans in a wire-mesh steamer basket; place on rack.

2 Lock lid; set pressure release valve to Sealing. Select Pressure Cook. Select High Pressure; set timer for 2 minutes.

3 When time is up, use quick release. Unlock lid. Remove steamer basket

Roasted Beet Salad

The earthiness of the beets is complemented by the slight sweetness of fennel.

START TO FINISH 25 minutes (10 minutes active)

SERVINGS 6

INGREDIENTS

- 8 medium beets, unpeeled
- 3 tablespoons honey
- 3 tablespoons balsamic vinegar
- 3 tablespoons olive oil
- 1/2 teaspoon kosher salt
- 1/4 teaspoon ground black pepper
- 2 cups lettuce, chopped
- 1 large shallot, minced
- 1 bulb fennel, thinly sliced
- 1/2 cup toasted pecans
- 1/4 cup crumbled blue cheese
  Garnish: fennel fronds

1 Remove leafy green stalks and roots from beets, being careful not to cut skin.

2 In an Instant Pot, place a steam rack; add 1 cup water. Place beets on rack.

3 Lock lid; set pressure release valve to Sealing. Select Pressure Cook. Select High Pressure; set timer for 15 minutes.

4 When time is up, use quick release. Unlock lid.

5 Using tongs, place beets in a bowl to cool for about 10 minutes, then run them under cool water. Using a paper towel, scrub off skin. Cut beets into 1/2-inch pieces.

6 To make beet dressing, in a small bowl, whisk together honey, balsamic vinegar, olive oil, salt and pepper.

7 On a serving platter, spread lettuce; top with beets, shallot, fennel slices, pecans and blue cheese. Drizzle with dressing; garnish with fennel fronds.

Orange Glazed Carrots

Make this dish more colorful by using baby carrots in a variety of hues. Leave the tops on; they're both edible and decorative.

START TO FINISH 15 minutes
(5 minutes active)

SERVINGS 6

INGREDIENTS

- 2 pounds whole baby carrots with tops
- ½ cup brown sugar
- ½ cup fresh orange juice
- 3 tablespoons butter
- 1 teaspoon cinnamon
- 1 tablespoon orange zest
- ½ teaspoon salt
- 1 tablespoon cornstarch
- ¼ cup water
- Garnish: mint leaves

1 In an Instant Pot, add carrots and next 6 ingredients.

2 Lock lid; set pressure release valve to Sealing. Select Pressure Cook. Select High Pressure; set timer for 3 minutes.

3 When time is up, use quick release. Unlock lid.

4 Select Sauté; bring mixture to a boil.

5 In a small bowl, whisk together cornstarch and water. Gradually stir into carrot mixture.

6 Cook and stir until thickened, about 2 minutes.

7 Serve, garnished with mint leaves.

Succotash With Edamame

Bacon adds some extra flavor to this savory mix of corn and edamame.

START TO FINISH 25 minutes
(15 minutes active)

SERVINGS 6-8

INGREDIENTS

- 4 slices bacon, chopped
- 1 cup coarsely chopped red sweet pepper
- ½ cup chopped red onion
- 2 cloves garlic, minced
- 1 (16-ounce) package frozen corn kernels
- 2 cups frozen shelled edamame
- ½ cup chicken broth
- 1½ cups cherry tomatoes, halved
- ½ cup chopped fresh basil
  Salt and ground black pepper

1 On an Instant Pot, select Sauté; add bacon. Cook, stirring occasionally, until bacon is crisp, about 5 minutes. Use a slotted spoon to transfer bacon to a paper towel-lined plate.

2 Add red pepper, onion and garlic. Cook in bacon drippings, stirring occasionally, until softened, about 3 minutes. Select Cancel.

3 Stir in corn, edamame and chicken broth. Lock lid; set pressure release valve to Sealing. Select Pressure Cook. Select High Pressure; set timer for 5 minutes. When time is up, use quick release. Unlock lid.

4 Stir in tomatoes, bacon and basil. Season to taste with salt and pepper to serve.

Braised Parsnips & Carrots With Rosemary

Parsnips are a root vegetable and a close cousin to carrots, so it makes sense that the two pair perfectly together in this simple side dish.

START TO FINISH 25 minutes
(15 minutes active)

SERVINGS 4

INGREDIENTS

- ¾ pound parsnips, peeled and cut into ½-inch diagonal slices
- ¾ pound carrots, peeled and cut into ½-inch diagonal slices
- ¼ cup vegetable or chicken broth
- ¼ cup white wine
- 2 teaspoons dried rosemary, lightly crushed
- 1 tablespoon butter
  Salt and ground black pepper

1 In an Instant Pot, add parsnips, carrots, broth, wine and rosemary.
2 Lock lid; set pressure release valve to Sealing. Select Pressure Cook. Select High Pressure; set timer for 4 minutes.
3 When time is up, use quick release. Unlock lid.
4 Add butter; toss gently to coat. Season to taste with salt and pepper.
5 Transfer to a bowl and serve.

Steamed Asparagus With Hollandaise Sauce

If you don't want to make hollandaise from scratch, ready-made and mix versions are available.

START TO FINISH 15 minutes
(3 minutes active)

SERVINGS 4

INGREDIENTS

- 1 pound fresh asparagus, tough ends trimmed
- 1 cup chicken broth
  Sea salt
  Cracked black pepper
  Hollandaise sauce

1 In an Instant Pot, place rack.
2 Place asparagus on rack. Pour in broth.

Rainbow Garlic Potatoes

3 Lock lid; set pressure release valve to Sealing. Select Pressure Cook. Select High Pressure; set timer for 2 minutes.
4 When time is up, use quick release. Unlock lid.
5 Remove asparagus to serving platter; season with salt and pepper and serve with sauce.

Rainbow Garlic Potatoes

The different potato varieties each has their own subtle flavor.

START TO FINISH 25 minutes
(10 minutes active)

SERVINGS 4-6

INGREDIENTS

- 3 tablespoons olive oil
- 3 tablespoons butter, melted
- 1 small onion, cut into 8 wedges
- 5 cloves garlic, minced
- 1½ pounds assorted colorful potatoes, sliced in half*
- ¾ cup chicken broth
  Salt and pepper

1 On an Instant Pot, select Sauté; heat oil and butter. When butter is melted and foaming, add onion, garlic and potatoes. Cook and stir for 5 minutes. Select Cancel. Pour in broth. Season to taste with salt and pepper.
2 Lock lid; set pressure release valve to Sealing. Select Pressure Cook. Select High Pressure; set timer for 6 minutes.
3 When time is up, use natural release. Unlock lid.
4 Use a slotted spoon to transfer potatoes and onions to serving bowl.
*TIP Use any combination of potatoes. Cut into equal-size chunks of 2 to 3 inches for even cooking.

QUICK TIP

Bags of mixed-color baby potatoes are sold in many supermarkets so you can grab just one bag instead of multiple bags.

Sesame Broccoli

Add a little Asian flavor to your dinner. Or try a different version, using hazelnut oil; substitute chopped hazelnuts for the sesame seeds.

START TO FINISH 10 minutes (2 minutes active)

SERVINGS 2

INGREDIENTS

  2 teaspoons sesame oil
  1 (12-ounce) bag broccoli florets
  1 teaspoon salt
 ½ teaspoon red pepper flakes
 ⅓ cup water
    Garnish: sesame seeds

1 On an Instant Pot, select Sauté; heat oil and stir in florets.
2 Sprinkle with salt and pepper flakes. Stir for 1 minute.
3 Lock lid; set pressure release valve to Sealing. Select Pressure Cook. Select High Pressure; set timer for 1 minute.
4 When time is up, use natural release for 5 minutes, then quick-release remaining pressure. Unlock lid.
5 Place broccoli on serving plate; garnish with sesame seeds.

Sweet Corn With Garlic-Basil Butter

Try this with fresh-picked corn at the height of summer!

START TO FINISH 15 minutes (10 minutes active)

SERVINGS 4

INGREDIENTS

- 4 ears corn, shucked
- ¼ cup butter, softened
- ½ teaspoon dried basil
- ½ teaspoon garlic powder
- ⅛ teaspoon salt
- ⅛ teaspoon ground black pepper

1 In an Instant Pot, place a steam rack. Pour in 1 cup water. Place corn on rack.

2 Lock lid; set pressure release valve to Sealing. Select Pressure Cook. Select High Pressure; set timer for 1 minute. When time is up, use quick release. Unlock lid.

3 Meanwhile, in a small bowl, mix remaining ingredients.

4 Brush corn with herb butter to serve.

Creamy Mashed
Potatoes

Creamy Mashed Potatoes

You'll find yourself turning to this simple recipe for fluffy potatoes as a side dish for many recipes in this book.

START TO FINISH 20 minutes
(5 minutes active)

SERVINGS 8

INGREDIENTS

- 6 large russet potatoes, peeled and quartered
- 2 teaspoons salt
- 1/2 teaspoon ground black pepper
- 1/2 cup butter
- 1 cup milk
- 1/2 cup heavy cream
  Garnishes: butter pats, snipped chives

1 In an Instant Pot, place a steam rack. Pour in 1 cup water. Place potatoes on rack.

2 Lock lid; set pressure release valve to Sealing. Select Pressure Cook. Select High Pressure; set timer for 8 minutes.

3 When time is up, use natural release for 5 minutes, then quick-release remaining pressure. Unlock lid.

4 In a large bowl, use a potato masher or an immersion blender to mash potatoes with salt, pepper, butter and milk to desired consistency.

5 Slowly stir in heavy cream to reach desired consistency. Garnish with butter pats and chives.

Fresh Creamed Corn

Fresh Creamed Corn

Be sure to use sweet yellow corn
for the best results in this classic
side dish. Many supermarkets
carry frozen ears of corn or precut
kernels, so you can make this dish
year-round.

START TO FINISH 10 minutes
(5 minutes active)

SERVINGS 4

INGREDIENTS

- 4 ears yellow corn, scraped
- ¼ cup butter
- 1 (8-ounce) cream cheese, cubed
- 1 teaspoon sugar
- ½ cup half-and-half
- ¼ cup heavy cream
- 1 teaspoon salt
- 1 teaspoon ground black pepper
  Garnishes: cracked black
  pepper, thyme sprigs

1 In an Instant Pot, add all
ingredients.
2 Lock lid; set pressure release valve
to Sealing. Select Pressure Cook.
Select High Pressure; set timer for
4 minutes.
3 When time is up, use natural
release for 5 minutes, then
quick-release remaining pressure.
Unlock lid.
4 Garnish, as desired.

Sweet Potatoes With Pumpkin Pie Butter

Two classic fall flavors join together for a smooth, sweet and creamy dish.

START TO FINISH 30 minutes
(10 minutes active)

SERVINGS 8

INGREDIENTS

4	medium sweet potatoes, peeled and cut into 2-inch chunks
½	cup butter, softened
3	tablespoons brown sugar
1½	teaspoons pumpkin pie spice
½	teaspoon salt

1 In an Instant Pot, place a vegetable steamer; pour in 1 cup water. Place potatoes in basket.

2 Lock lid; set pressure release valve to Sealing. Select Pressure Cook. Select High Pressure; set timer for 10 minutes.

3 When time is up, use natural release. Unlock lid.

4 In a small bowl mix butter, brown sugar and pumpkin pie spice.

5 Using a potato masher, mash potatoes with salt and pumpkin pie butter to desired consistency.

6 Top with butter pats to serve.

QUICK TIP

If you don't have pumpkin pie spice, substitute apple pie spice— or use a combination of ½ teaspoon each of cinnamon and ginger and ¼ teaspoon each of nutmeg and allspice.

**Salt-Crusted Potatoes
With Butter Dipping Sauce**

Salt-Crusted Potatoes With Butter Dipping Sauce

These taters originated in upstate New York as salt mine workers' lunches.

START TO FINISH 20 minutes
(5 minutes active)

SERVINGS 6

INGREDIENTS

- 2 pounds small whole potatoes*
- 8 cups water
- 1 cup salt
    Melted butter

1 In an Instant Pot, add potatoes, water and salt.

2 Lock lid; set pressure release valve to Sealing. Select Pressure Cook. Select High Pressure; set timer for 8 minutes.

3 When time is up, use natural release. Unlock lid.

4 Drain potatoes in a colander. Let potatoes sit in the colander for about 5 minutes to dry the skins so some of the salt crystallizes on the skins.

5 Serve with butter on the side.

*TIP Don't cut the potatoes. The skins prevent absorption of too much salt.

All-Purpose Marinara Sauce

Pour this classic vegetable-based sauce over meatballs or plain pasta.

START TO FINISH 30 minutes
(10 minutes active)

SERVINGS 6

INGREDIENTS

- ¼ cup good-quality olive oil
- 1 medium onion, chopped
- 2 to 3 garlic cloves, minced
- 1 (28-ounce) can crushed or diced tomatoes
- 1 (6-ounce) can tomato paste
- 1 teaspoon sugar
- 1 red bell pepper, chopped
- 2 carrots, grated
- 1 teaspoon dried oregano, crushed
- 1 bay leaf
- 8 ounces sliced mushrooms (optional)
- ½ teaspoon sea salt or kosher salt
- ¼ teaspoon ground black pepper
- ½ cup fresh basil, snipped

All-Purpose Marinara Sauce

1 On an Instant Pot, select Sauté; heat oil. Add onion and garlic; sauté for 5 minutes. Select Cancel. Stir in tomatoes, tomato paste, sugar, bell pepper, carrots, oregano, bay leaf, mushrooms (if using), salt and pepper.

2 Lock lid; set pressure release valve to Sealing. Select Pressure Cook. Select High Pressure; set timer for 6 minutes.

3 When time is up, use quick release. Unlock lid. Remove bay leaf and stir in fresh basil.

4 Serve over pasta, or use in any recipe that calls for marinara sauce.

NOTE If you have a large Instant Pot, double the recipe and freeze half of it. It stores well for up to 3 months in the freezer; just defrost overnight in the fridge then heat on the stove.

Quick & Easy Salsa

No need to buy salsa in jars; this recipe is simple and customizable to your spiciness preference.

START TO FINISH 20 minutes
(5 minutes active)

SERVINGS 6

INGREDIENTS

- 8 large tomatoes, roughly chopped
- 6 garlic cloves, diced
- 2 jalapeño peppers, seeded and diced
- 1 green bell pepper, diced
- 1 small red onion, diced
- 1 small yellow onion, diced
- 3 teaspoon kosher salt
- ½ teaspoon freshly ground black pepper
- ½ teaspoon baking soda
- ¼ cup tomato paste
- 2 tablespoons lime juice
    Garnish: cilantro leaves

1 In an Instant Pot, stir together tomatoes, garlic, jalapeños, bell pepper, onions, salt, pepper and baking soda.

2 Lock lid; set pressure release valve to Sealing. Select Pressure Cook. Select High Pressure; set timer for 5 minutes.

3 When time is up, use natural release for 10 minutes, then quick-release remaining pressure. Unlock lid.

4 Stir in tomato paste and lime juice. Let cool completely before serving. Garnish with cilantro.

Melting Potatoes

Yukon gold potatoes are essential in this recipe—they ensure a creamy, melted texture.

START TO FINISH 30 minutes
(20 minutes active)

SERVINGS 4

INGREDIENTS

- 6 tablespoons butter
- 1 teaspoon salt
- 1 teaspoon ground black pepper
- 2 tablespoons thyme leaves
- 1 pound Yukon gold potatoes, cut into 1-inch slices
- 1 teaspoon chopped garlic
- $\frac{1}{2}$ cup chicken broth
  Garnishes: sea salt, chopped parsley

1 On an Instant Pot, select Sauté; add butter, salt, pepper and thyme. Cook for 2 minutes.

2 Add potato slices in an even layer; cook for 5 minutes per side. Remove potatoes from pot.

3 Add garlic to pot. Place a steam rack inside pot. Place potatoes on rack; pour broth over the top.

4 Lock lid; set pressure release valve to Sealing. Select Pressure Cook. Select High Pressure; set timer for 1 minute.

5 When time is up, use natural release for 10 minutes, then quick-release remaining pressure. Unlock lid. Remove potatoes.

6 Select Sauté; cook liquid until reduced, about 2 minutes.

7 Return potatoes to pot; cook for 3 minutes per side.

8 Place potato slices on a serving plate; garnish, as desired.

QUICK TIP

Substitute orange liqueur for some of the orange juice in this sauce. Just a bit of Cointreau or Grand Marnier makes a flavorful upgrade.

Cranberry-Orange Sauce

Cranberry-Orange Sauce

If you can find blood oranges at your market, pick some up! Their juice is terrific in this recipe (and in adult beverages). Some stores sell fresh-squeezed blood orange juice, which is almost as good.

START TO FINISH 25 minutes
(5 minutes active)

SERVINGS 12

INGREDIENTS

- 2 (12-ounce) bags fresh or frozen cranberries, washed
- 2/3 cups sugar
- 1/2 cup freshly squeezed orange or blood orange juice
- 1 cinnamon stick
- 1/4 teaspoon nutmeg
- 1/4 teaspoon vanilla extract
  Garnish: blood orange or navel orange slices

1 In an Instant Pot, add cranberries and next 4 ingredients.
2 Lock lid; set pressure release valve to Sealing. Select Pressure Cook. Select High Pressure; set timer for 5 minutes.
3 When time is up, use natural release for 15 minutes, then quick-release remaining pressure. Unlock lid.
4 Remove cinnamon stick. Stir in vanilla.
5 Garnish, as desired.

Red Cabbage With Bacon

This side, served with some grilled or broiled pork chops, is a match that was meant to be!

START TO FINISH 30 minutes
(10 minutes active)

SERVINGS 4

INGREDIENTS

- 1 tablespoon olive oil
- 1 small onion, chopped
- 3 slices bacon, chopped
- 1 Granny Smith apple, coarsely chopped
- 5 cups chopped red cabbage
- 1 cup chicken broth
- 1/2 cup apple cider vinegar

- 1/2 teaspoon kosher salt
- 1/4 cup crumbled feta cheese
  Curly parsley

1 On an Instant Pot, select Sauté. Heat oil; add onion and sauté for 3 to 5 minutes until translucent. Add bacon; cook, stirring constantly, for 3 minutes or until bacon begins to crisp.
2 Add apple pieces and cabbage to pot; stir in broth and vinegar.
3 Lock lid; set pressure release valve to Sealing. Select Pressure Cook. Select High Pressure; set timer for 10 minutes.
4 When time is up, use quick release. Unlock lid.
5 Using a slotted spoon, place cabbage on serving plate; sprinkle with salt and toss. Let cool 10 minutes. Sprinkle with feta cheese and parsley; serve warm.

Gorgonzola Asparagus

Walnuts add a delightful crunchy contrast to the creamy, salty cheese. Use any blue cheese you like.

START TO FINISH 6 minutes
(5 minutes active)

SERVINGS 4

INGREDIENTS

- 1 pound asparagus spears, trimmed
- 2 teaspoons olive oil
- 1 tablespoon balsamic vinegar
- 2 tablespoons crumbled gorgonzola cheese
- 2 tablespoons chopped, toasted walnuts

1 In an Instant Pot, add 1 cup water. Place asparagus evenly in steamer basket; place basket in pot. Lock lid.
2 Set pressure release valve to Sealing. Select Pressure Cook; set timer for 1 minute.
3 When time is up, use quick release. Unlock lid.
4 Transfer asparagus to a bowl; toss with the oil and vinegar. Place on a serving plate; sprinkle with gorgonzola cheese and walnuts.

Sautéed Spinach

Sautéed Spinach

Bacon, onion and garlic pack some major flavor in this dish! Use fresh baby spinach if you can find it, or tear larger leaves into pieces.

START TO FINISH 15 minutes (10 minutes active)

SERVINGS 4

INGREDIENTS

1 tablespoon olive oil

4 slices bacon, sliced

1 small onion, chopped

1 tablespoon minced garlic

8 cups fresh spinach

2 cups chicken broth

1 teaspoon salt

1/2 teaspoon ground black pepper

1 On an Instant Pot, select Sauté; heat oil. Add bacon, onion and garlic. Cook for 3 minutes.

2 Add spinach, broth, salt and pepper.

3 Lock lid; set pressure release valve to Sealing. Select Pressure Cook. Select High Pressure; set timer for 4 minutes.

4 When time is up, use natural release for 5 minutes. Unlock lid; place spinach on serving platter.

Brussels Sprouts With Bacon

Quickly steaming sprouts makes them tender and allows them to retain their glorious colors.

START TO FINISH 15 minutes (5 minutes active)

SERVINGS 4

INGREDIENTS

1 pound fresh Brussels sprouts (both purple and green), trimmed and halved

1 tablespoon olive oil

1 tablespoon chopped garlic

1 small onion, chopped

4 slices bacon, chopped

1/2 teaspoon salt

1/2 teaspoon ground black pepper

1 Pour 1 cup of water into Instant Pot. Place steamer basket inside.

2 Arrange Brussels sprouts in basket.

3 Lock lid; set pressure release valve to Sealing. Select Pressure Cook. Select High Pressure; set timer for 3 minutes.

4 When time is up, use quick release. Unlock lid.

5 Remove Brussels sprouts from pot and place in colander to drain.

6 Select Sauté; heat oil. Add garlic and onion; cook for 2 minutes. Add bacon and cook for 5 minutes.

7 Add sprouts back to pot to heat through, stirring well to coat. Serve immediately.

Brussels Sprouts
With Bacon

QUICK TIP

Purple Brussels
sprouts are an heirloom
variety; they're sweeter
than the green ones.
Look for them at
farmers markets.

DESSERTS

END YOUR MEAL ON A SWEET NOTE
WITH THESE TEMPTING TREATS.
WHEN MADE IN THE INSTANT POT,
THEY'RE READY IN NO TIME!

"Baked" Stuffed
Apples, page 137

Rice Pudding

There's a good reason why this old-school dessert is still popular today!

START TO FINISH 30 minutes
(5 minutes active)

SERVINGS 4

INGREDIENTS

- 1 cup arborio rice
- 2 cups half-and-half
- 1 cup water
- $\frac{2}{3}$ cup granulated sugar
- $\frac{1}{3}$ cup raisins
- 1 teaspoon vanilla extract
- 1 teaspoon ground cinnamon
- $\frac{1}{8}$ teaspoon ground nutmeg
  Pinch salt
  Ground nutmeg

1 In an Instant Pot, stir together all ingredients except nutmeg.

2 Lock lid. Set pressure release valve to Sealing. Select Pressure Cook. Select High Pressure; set timer for 5 minutes.

3 When time is up, use natural release for 10 minutes, then quick-release remaining pressure. Unlock lid.

4 Stir pudding and let sit for 5 to 10 minutes to thicken up.

5 Divide pudding between 4 serving bowls; sprinkle with nutmeg to serve.

Express Peach Cobbler

Using only a few ingredients, you can have a sweet treat in just 30 minutes.

START TO FINISH 30 minutes
(10 minutes active)

SERVINGS 6

INGREDIENTS

- 1 stick butter, melted
- 1 cup granulated sugar
- 1 cup baking mix (like Bisquick)
- 1 cup milk
- 1 (21-ounce) can peach pie filling

1 In an Instant Pot, pour butter.

2 In a large bowl, whisk together sugar, baking mix and milk; pour into pot.

3 Pour pie filling over batter; do not mix.

4 Lock lid; set pressure release valve to Sealing. Select Pressure Cook. Select High Pressure; set timer for 15 minutes.

5 When time is up, use quick release. Unlock lid.

6 Serve warm.

Apple Crisp

You can substitute your favorite apple variety for the Honeycrisps.

START TO FINISH 20 minutes
(10 minutes active)
SERVINGS 4

INGREDIENTS

- 3 cups chopped Honeycrisp apples
- 2 teaspoons plus 3 tablespoons honey, divided
- 1/2 teaspoon cinnamon
- 2 teaspoons lemon juice
- 1/4 cup melted butter
- 1/3 cup rolled oats
- 1/3 cup all-purpose flour
- 1/4 teaspoon cinnamon
- 1/4 teaspoon kosher salt
  Vanilla ice cream
  Caramel sauce

1 In a large bowl, combine apples, 2 teaspoons honey, cinnamon and lemon juice. Set aside.
2 In a small bowl, whisk together butter and remaining honey. Stir in oats, flour, cinnamon and salt.
3 Add apple mixture to Instant Pot; top evenly with oat mixture.
4 Lock lid; set pressure release valve to Sealing. Select Pressure Cook. Select High Pressure; set timer for 7 minutes.
5 When time is up, use quick release. Unlock lid.
6 Serve warm with vanilla ice cream and caramel sauce.

"Baked" Stuffed Apples

This gluten-free dessert is popular at holiday time but delicious all year.

START TO FINISH 30 minutes
(15 minutes active)
SERVINGS 4

INGREDIENTS

- 1/2 cup dried cranberries
- 3 tablespoons chopped walnuts
- 3 tablespoons pure maple syrup
- 1 tablespoon very soft butter
- 3/4 teaspoon pumpkin pie spice
- 4 large apples, like Honeycrisp or other sweet crisp variety, cored
- 1 cup dry red wine
- 1/2 cup sugar

1 In a small bowl, combine cranberries, walnuts, maple syrup, butter and pumpkin pie spice. Stuff an equal amount into apple cores.
2 In an Instant Pot, place apples; pour in wine and sprinkle sugar around base of apples.
3 Lock lid; set pressure release valve to Sealing. Select Pressure Cook. Select High Pressure; set timer for 10 minutes. When time is up, use quick release. Unlock lid.
4 Place apples in individual serving bowls; pour over cooking liquid.

3 SPEEDY SWEET ACCENTS

Whip Up a Quick Fruit Sauce

Compotes make versatile desserts. Enjoy them over ice cream, angel food cake or toasted pound cake.

MIXED BERRY

Combine 1 pound each trimmed and halved strawberries and blueberries in Instant Pot. Stir in 1/4 cup sugar, 2 teaspoons orange juice and 1/2 teaspoon vanilla extract. Cook at high pressure for 1 minute. Use natural release. Let cool to thicken.

PEACH

Combine 2 pounds chopped fresh peaches, 1/4 cup sugar, 2 teaspoons orange juice and 1/2 teaspoon ground cinnamon in Instant Pot. Follow cooking instructions for Mixed Berry.

RASPBERRY-CHERRY

Combine 1 pound each raspberries and pitted tart cherries (frozen, thawed) in Instant Pot. Stir in 1/3 cup sugar, 2 teaspoons lemon juice, and 1/2 teaspoon vanilla extract. Follow cooking instructions for Mixed Berry.

Mocha Lava Cakes

Heat up some ooey, gooey goodness, perfect to serve solo or to share.

START TO FINISH 30 minutes
(10 minutes active)

SERVINGS 6

INGREDIENTS

   Softened butter
1 cup semisweet chocolate chips
½ cup butter
1 cup powdered sugar
3 whole eggs
3 egg yolks
½ cup all-purpose flour
1 teaspoon instant coffee granules

1 Butter six 6-ounce ramekins with softened butter; set aside. In a medium glass bowl, add chocolate chips and ½ cup butter; microwave on high for 1 minute or until butter is melted. Whisk until chocolate is completely melted; stir in sugar. Add whole eggs and egg yolks; mix well. Stir in flour and coffee granules. Spoon into prepared ramekins.

2 In an Instant Pot, pour 1 cup water. Place 3 filled ramekins in the water.

Place a steam rack over ramekins and place remaining ramekins on rack, positioning them so there is as little overlapping of the lower level with the upper level as possible.

3 Lock lid; set pressure release valve to Sealing. Select Pressure Cook. Select High Pressure; set timer for 15 minutes.

4 When time is up, use quick release. Unlock lid.

5 Let stand for 5 minutes before serving. (Or, for a gooey center, serve immediately. The cake will continue cooking as you let it rest, so the interior will solidify.)

Chocolate Chip
Mini Muffins

Chocolate Chip Mini Muffins

Serve this treat for brunch, dessert or anytime you want a little sweet.

START TO FINISH 35 minutes
(10 minutes active)

SERVINGS 6

INGREDIENTS

Vegetable cooking spray
2 tablespoon butter, softened
$^2/_3$ cup sugar
2 large eggs
1 teaspoon vanilla extract
1 cup all-purpose flour
$^1/_2$ teaspoon kosher salt
$^1/_2$ teaspoon baking soda
$^3/_4$ cup mini chocolate chips

1 In an Instant Pot, place steam rack. Pour in 1 cup water. Spray an Instant Pot-friendly mini muffin mold with vegetable cooking spray.
2 In a medium bowl using an electric mixer, cream butter and sugar. Beat in eggs and vanilla. Fold in flour, salt and baking soda. Stir it chocolate chips. Pour mixture into mold.
3 Place mold on rack; cover loosely with foil. Lock lid; set pressure release valve to Sealing. Select Pressure Cook. Select High Pressure; set timer for 20 minutes.
4 When time is up, use natural release for 10 minutes, then quick-release remaining pressure. Unlock lid.
5 Let the muffins cool in the mold.

Pumpkin Creme Brulee

You'll love this twist on the classic!

START TO FINISH 35 minutes
(10 minutes active)

SERVINGS 4

INGREDIENTS

4 egg yolks
$^1/_2$ cup granulated sugar, divided
1 cup heavy cream
$^1/_2$ cup pure pumpkin puree
$^1/_4$ teaspoon pumpkin spice
$^1/_2$ teaspoon vanilla bean paste
$^1/_8$ teaspoon kosher salt
Garnishes: candied pecans, whipped cream

1 In a large bowl, whisk together yolks and $^1/_4$ cup sugar until sugar is dissolved. Whisk in cream, pumpkin puree, pumpkin spice, vanilla bean paste and salt until combined.
2 Using a fine mesh strainer, strain mixture and divide evenly between 4 ramekins. Cover each with foil.
3 In an Instant Pot, place steam rack. Pour in 2 cups water. Place ramekins on rack.
4 Lock lid; set pressure release valve to Sealing. Select Pressure Cook. Select High Pressure; set timer for 6 minutes.
5 When time is up, use natural release. Unlock lid; place ramekins on cooling rack. When cool, refrigerate for 3 hours.
6 Just before serving, sprinkle remaining sugar on each ramekin; using a kitchen torch or broiler, melt sugar until golden. Top with garnishes.

Warm Indian Pudding With Ice Cream

This baked custard is a holiday classic in New England.

START TO FINISH 45 minutes
(10 minutes active)

SERVINGS 6

INGREDIENTS

2 cups whole milk
$^1/_2$ cup yellow cornmeal
1 teaspoon pumpkin pie spice
$^1/_8$ teaspoon salt
1 tablespoon butter, softened
1 (12-ounce) package frozen pureed winter squash, thawed
$^1/_4$ cup brown sugar
2 tablespoons molasses
Vanilla ice cream

1 Whisk together milk, cornmeal, pumpkin pie spice and salt. Stir in butter, squash, brown sugar and molasses. Pour into a greased 1-quart casserole dish.
2 In an Instant Pot, place steam rack; pour in 1$^1/_2$ cups water. Fold an 18-inch-long piece of foil into thirds lengthwise. Place under casserole dish and use the two sides as a sling to place casserole on rack.
3 Lock lid; set pressure release valve to Sealing. Select Pressure Cook. Select High Pressure; set timer for 10 minutes.
4 When time is up, use natural release. Unlock lid.
5 Cool pudding on a wire rack for 15 to 20 minutes.
6 Serve warm with vanilla ice cream.

QUICK TIP

Molasses comes in various depths of flavor—light, dark and blackstrap. For the most intense molasses flavor, choose blackstrap.

Warm Indian Pudding With Ice Cream

RECIPE INDEX

*Indicates recipes that are 30+ minutes (but worth the extra time!)

Apple Crisp,
page 137

CREDITS
PHOTOGRAPHY
Liam Franklin

ADDITIONAL PHOTOGRAPHY
Ken Carlson   Photography
Joshua Hake   Food Stylist
Trish Myers   Assistant Food Stylist
[5, 16, 20–21, 24, 28, 42, 52–53, 54–55,
57, 79, 92, 97, 116, 117, 120–121, 122–123,
124–125, 132–133, 138–139, 141]

CENTENNIAL BOOKS

An Imprint of
Centennial Media, LLC
1111 Brickell Avenue, 10th Floor
Miami, FL 33131, U.S.A.

ISBN 978-1-951274-87-0

Distributed by
Simon & Schuster, Inc.
1230 Avenue of the Americas
New York, NY 10020, U.S.A.

For information about custom editions, special sales and premium and corporate purchases, please contact Centennial Media at contact@centennialmedia.com.

Manufactured in China

10 9 8 7 6 5 4 3 2 1

Publishers & Co-Founders Ben Harris, Sebastian Raatz
Editorial Director Annabel Vered
Creative Director Jessica Power
Executive Editor Janet Giovanelli
Features Editor Alyssa Shaffer
Deputy Editors Ron Kelly, Anne Marie O'Connor
Managing Editor Lisa Chambers
Design Director Martin Elfers
Senior Art Director Pino Impastato
Art Directors Runyon Hall, Jaclyn Loney, Natali Suasnavas, Joseph Ulatowski
Copy/Production Patty Carroll, Angela Taormina
Senior Photo Editor Jenny Veiga
Production Manager Paul Rodina
Production Assistant Alyssa Swiderski
Editorial Assistant Tiana Schippa
Sales & Marketing Jeremy Nurnberg